SINGER

SEWING REFERENCE LIBRARY™

Sewing Essentials

Cy DeCosse Incorporated
Minnetonka, Minnesota

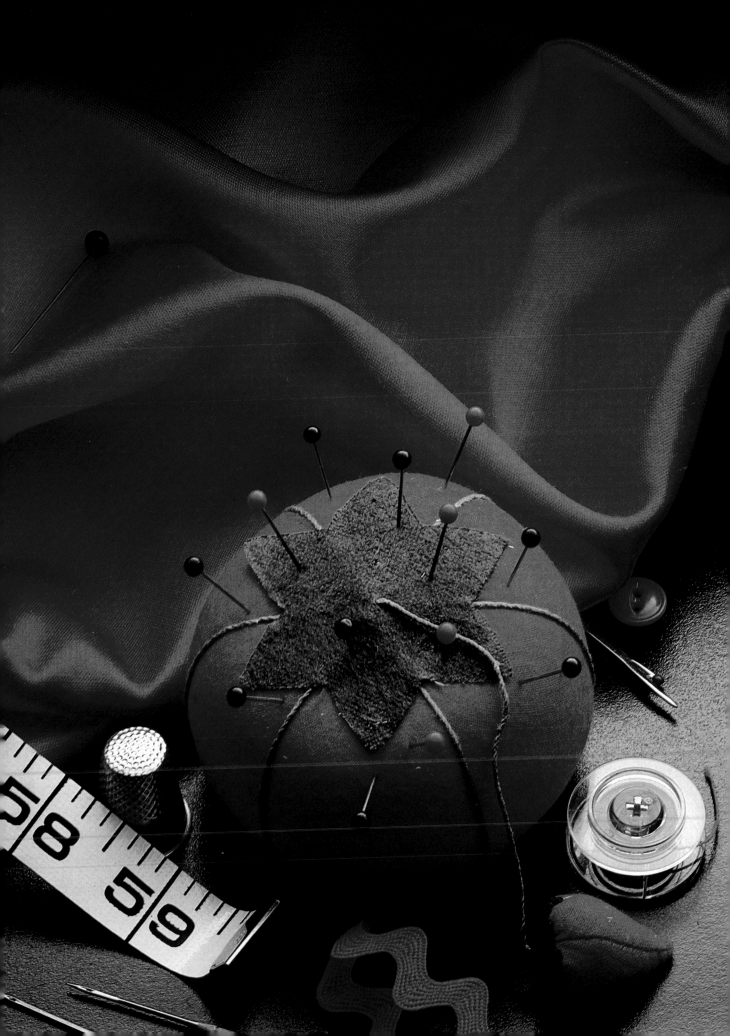

SINGER

◆ SEWING REFERENCE LIBRARY™ ◆

Sewing Essentials

Contents

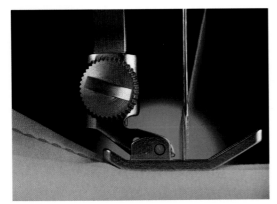

Also available from the publisher: *Sewing for the Home, Clothing Care & Repair, Sewing for Style, Sewing Specialty Fabrics, Sewing Activewear, The Perfect Fit, Timesaving Sewing.*

Library of Congress Cataloging in Publication Data

Sewing Essentials

(Singer Sewing Reference Library)
Includes index. 1. Sewing I. Series.
TT705.S47 1984
646.2   84-42637
ISBN 0-86573-201-9
ISBN 0-86573-202-7 (pbk.)

Distributed by: Contemporary Books, Inc., Chicago, Illinois

CY DE COSSE INCORPORATED
Chairman: Cy DeCosse
President: James B. Maus
Executive Vice President: William B. Jones

SEWING ESSENTIALS
Created by: The Editors of Cy DeCosse Incorporated, in cooperation with the Singer Consumer Education Department. SINGER is a trademark of The Singer Company and is used under license.

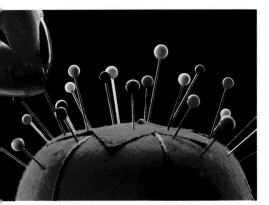

Project Director: Gail Devens
Editor: Christine Kittleson
Art Director: Susan Schultz
Project Manager: Bernice Maehren
Writers: Gail Devens, Betty Braden,
  Christine Kittleson
Director of Photography: Buck Holzemer
Staff Photographers: Jerry Robb, Jim Brown,
  Tony Kubat
Production Director: Christine Watkins

Production Staff: Douglas Meyers, Julie Churchill,
  Jean Sherlock, Jennie Smith, Nancy Nardone,
  Christopher Lentz, Michelle Alexander
Consultants: Zoe Graul, The Singer Company;
  Janet Hethorn, University of Minnesota;
  Kathy Alme, American Sewing Guild; Gerry
  Robins, Cranston Print Works; Angela Ariss
Sewing Staff: Phyllis Galbraith, Bridget Haugh,
  Carol Neumann, Julie Huber

Garment Construction: Wendy Fedie,
  Lorna Kittleson, Lynn Lohmann,
  Nancy Lohmann, Jill Crum
Contributing Manufacturers: The Singer
  Company; B. Blumenthal and Company;
  Coats & Clark; Risdon Corporation; Marks
  International, Inc.; Dyno Merchandise
  Corporation
Color Separations: Weston Engraving Co., Inc.
Printing: R. R. Donnelley & Sons Co. (1187)

How to Use This Book

Like any other art or craft, sewing begins with basic techniques. This book gives you the essential information that every sewer needs to know.

To prepare *Sewing Essentials*, the editors interviewed sewing experts, sewing teachers, students, beginning and experienced sewers, industry seamstresses, designers and professional dressmakers from all over the country. We asked them what they considered to be the most important principles and techniques for successful sewing.

Updated Basics

The people we interviewed all agreed that certain essential techniques have to be learned and perfected before a sewer advances to the next level of expertise. They also agreed that it is important to keep pace with changing methods and new technology to make the most efficient use of your sewing time. They emphasized using the newest timesaving tools and techniques without compromising on quality.

The first major consideration is sewing equipment. New tools and sewing aids have made sewing faster and easier than ever. Many sewing machines now have automatic capabilities for zigzag stitching, stretch stitches, buttonholes — even computer technology to program the stitches. Sewing machines can eliminate the time-consuming hand sewing that used to be necessary in garment construction. You can sew a garment entirely by machine, and you can save even more time by using new sewing aids like fabric glue, basting tape and fusible interfacing.

Much of this book is devoted to getting your sewing project off to a good start. The planning and decisions you make before you actually start sewing are just as important as the care you take in constructing the garment. Taking accurate measurements, choosing the right fabric for the pattern, buying the appropriate interfacing and notions — all of these steps affect the quality and fit of the finished product. Read through the tips and suggestions in the "Getting Started" section before you go to the fabric store. After you get home, take the time to prepare your fabric and follow the other procedures shown in the "Layout, Cutting & Marking" section.

A New Approach to Fundamental Techniques

The remainder of the book features the basic techniques you will use for nearly everything you sew. These are divided into five major sections: stitches, seams, shaping methods, outer edges and closures. Each is given an overview as well as a step-by-step description of how to achieve the best results. As you practice these fundamental techniques, they become part of your sewing repertoire, ready to apply on future sewing projects.

This is not a "project" book. It does not take you through the construction of a garment. Your pattern does that. This is a reference featuring new tips and methods, special techniques for certain fabrics and more detailed explanations of pattern instructions. The book gives you the opportunity to choose the best technique for your purposes. It emphasizes the details that make the difference between a professional-looking garment and one that looks homemade. Fashion details come and go, but the fundamentals of sewing can be applied to any design.

Step-by-Step Guidance

The photos add depth and dimension to the instructions, giving you a close-up look at each step. In some cases, the stitches are shown in heavier thread or a contrasting color to make them more visible. Some marking lines have also been exaggerated to show a particularly crucial matching point. These illustrative techniques should not be duplicated in your own sewing.

If you're just learning to sew or getting back to sewing, you may want to practice your skills on an easy project before starting an entire garment. Try sewing simple placemats and napkins to practice a seam or edge finish, a new hemming technique or the application of fusible interfacing. When you're ready to sew a garment, choose one of the simpler styles that are easy to fit, with fewer seams and details.

For the new sewer, the experienced sewer, or the sewer who has become a little rusty, this book is designed to be a help and an inspiration. Use it as your step-by-step guide to the satisfaction and fun of successful sewing.

Equipment

The Sewing Machine

A sewing machine is your most important piece of sewing equipment, so select one with care. A sturdy, well-built machine will give you many years of sewing enjoyment.

If you are buying a new machine, there are a variety of models available to fit any budget or sewing need. Types range from a basic zigzag with one or two built-in stitches, to the electronic machine that uses advanced computer technology to control and select the stitching.

Available features include built-in buttonholer, color-coded stitch selection, instant reverse, snap-on presser foot, free arm for stitching small round areas (such as pants legs), built-in bobbin winder, automatic tension and pressure adjustment, and automatic stitch length adjustment. Each feature usually adds to the cost of the machine, so look for a machine to match your sewing projects. Buy a machine that satisfies your sewing needs, but don't pay for features you will rarely use. Also consider the amount and difficulty of the sewing you do, and

the number of people you sew for. Talk to fabric store personnel and friends who sew. Ask for demonstrations, and try out and compare several models. Look for quality workmanship and ease of operation as well as stitching options.

The machine's cabinetry is another factor to consider. Portable machines offer the flexibility of moving to various work surfaces. Machines built into cabinets are designed to be the right height for sewing. They also help you stay organized by providing a convenient place to store sewing equipment and keep it handy.

Although sewing machines vary in capabilities and accessories, each has the same basic parts and controls. The equipment you will need for your machine is described on pages 14 and 15.

The principal parts of the sewing machine (opposite) are shown on a free-arm portable, but its basic parts are representative of all machines. Check your manual for specific location of these parts on your machine.

Machine Essentials

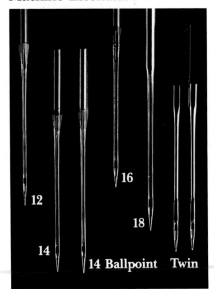

Needles are available in four basic types: *general-purpose* for a wide range of fabrics, in sizes 9/65 (finest) to 18/110; *ballpoint* for knits and stretch fabrics (size 9/65 to 16/100); *twin needle* for decorative stitching; and *wedge-point* (not shown) for leather and vinyl. Change the needle after sewing two to three garments or after hitting a pin. Damaged fabric is often caused by a bent, blunt or burred needle.

Thread for machine sewing comes in three weights: *extra fine* for lightweight fabrics and machine embroidery, *all-purpose* for general-purpose sewing, and *topstitching and buttonhole twist* for decorative and accent stitching. Thread should match the weight of the fabric and the size of the needle. For perfect tension, use the same size and type thread in the bobbin as you use in the needle.

Bobbins may be built-in or removable for winding. Bobbins with a built-in case are wound in the case. Removable bobbins have a removable bobbin case with a tension adjustment screw. They may be wound on the top or side of the machine. Start with an empty bobbin so the thread will wind evenly. Do not wind it too full or the bobbin thread will break.

Principal Parts of the Sewing Machine

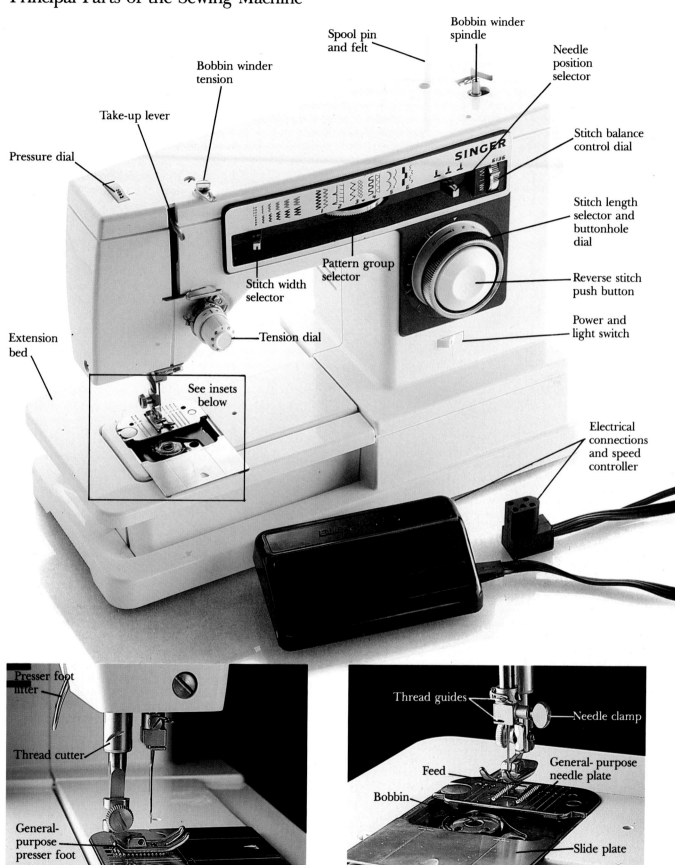

Spool pin and felt

Bobbin winder spindle

Bobbin winder tension

Needle position selector

Take-up lever

Stitch balance control dial

Pressure dial

SINGER

Stitch length selector and buttonhole dial

Pattern group selector

Stitch width selector

Reverse stitch push button

Tension dial

Power and light switch

Extension bed

See insets below

Electrical connections and speed controller

Presser foot lifter

Thread guides

Needle clamp

Thread cutter

General-purpose needle plate

Feed

General-purpose presser foot

Bobbin

Slide plate

Creating the Perfect Stitch

Perfect machine stitching is easy to achieve if you thread the machine properly and make the right adjustments in the stitch length, tension and pressure. These adjustments depend on your fabric and the kind of stitch desired. Consult your machine manual for threading procedures and location of controls.

The *stitch length regulator* is on either an inch scale from 0 to 20, a metric scale from 0 to 4, or a numerical scale from 0 to 9. For normal stitching, set the regulator at 10 to 12 stitches per inch, or at the number 3 for metric scale machines. On the numerical scale, higher numbers form a longer stitch; if a shorter stitch is desired, dial a lower number. An average stitch length is at number 5.

A perfect stitch depends on the delicate balance of pressure on the fabric, action of the feed, and tension on the stitch formation. In the ideal stitch, both top and bobbin thread are drawn equally into the fabric, and the link is formed midway between fabric layers.

The *stitch tension control* determines the amount of pressure on the threads as they pass through the machine. Too much pressure results in too little thread fed into the stitch. This causes the fabric to pucker. Too little pressure produces too much thread and a weak, loose stitch.

Adjust the *pressure regulator* for light pressure on lightweight fabrics, more pressure on heavy fabrics. Correct pressure ensures even feeding of the fabric layers during stitching. Some machines automatically adjust tension and pressure to the fabric.

Always check tension and pressure on a scrap of fabric before starting to sew. When experimenting with pressure and tension, thread the machine with different colors for top and bobbin thread to make the stitch links easier to see.

Straight Stitch Tension & Pressure

Correct tension and pressure makes stitches that are linked midway between the fabric layers. The stitches look even in length and tension on both sides. Fabric layers are fed evenly through the feed and fabric is not marred.

Too tight tension results in stitch links that are near the top layer of fabric. Fabric is puckered, and stitches are easily broken. Turn tension dial to a lower number. If pressure is too heavy, the bottom layer gathers up and may be damaged. Stitches may be uneven in length and tension. Dial pressure regulator to a lower number.

Too loose tension results in stitch links that are toward the bottom fabric layer. Seam is weak. Correct the problem by turning tension dial to a higher number. Too light pressure causes skipped and uneven stitches, and may pull fabric into the feed. Dial pressure regulator to a higher number.

Zigzag Stitch Tension & Pressure

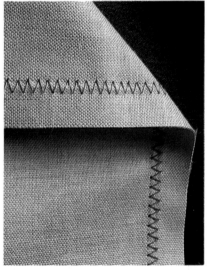

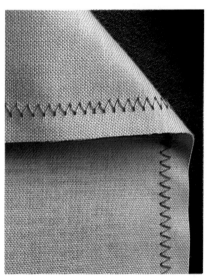

Correct tension and pressure in zigzag stitching produces stitches in which the interlocking link of threads falls at the corner of each stitch, midway between fabric layers. Stitches lie flat and fabric does not pucker.

Too tight tension causes fabric to pucker. The thread link falls near the top fabric layer. To correct, decrease the tension. Incorrect pressure is not as apparent in zigzag as in straight stitching. But if the pressure is not accurate, stitches will not be of even length.

Too loose tension causes the bottom layer to pucker and the thread link to fall near the bottom fabric layer. Increase tension to balance stitch. The zigzag stitch should be properly balanced in normal sewing. Loosen tension slightly for decorative stitches, and the top stitch pattern will become more rounded.

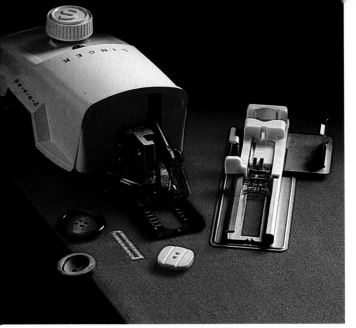

Machine Accessories for Special Tasks

Every sewing machine has accessories that allow it to perform a variety of special tasks. There are universal accessories that fit any machine, such as the zipper foot, buttonhole attachment and various hemming feet. Other accessories, such as a ruffler attachment, are designed to save time and effort for special types of sewing.

When adding a special accessory or foot to a machine you must know if your machine has a high shank, low shank or slanted shank. The *shank* is the distance from the bottom of the presser foot to the attachment screw. Attachments are specifically designed to fit one of these three styles.

The zigzag plate and the general-purpose foot usually come with the machine. Other accessories often included are the straight-stitch plate and foot, buttonhole foot or attachment, zipper foot, seam guide, various hemming feet, and Even Feed™ or roller foot. The machine manual explains how to attach the various accessories and achieve the best results with each.

Buttonhole attachments allow you to stitch complete buttonholes in a single step. One type stitches and adjusts the buttonhole length to fit the button placed in a carrier behind the foot. When the button is larger than 1½" (3.8 cm), or of an unusual shape or thickness, the gauge lines can be used instead of the carrier. Another type of buttonholer for straight-stitch machines makes buttonholes automatically using templates of various sizes. Keyhole buttonholes can be made with this accessory.

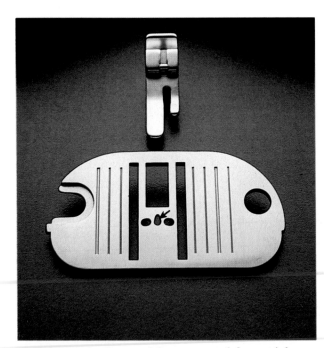

Straight-stitch plate and foot are used for straight stitching only. The needle hole (arrow) in the plate is small and round. The straight-stitch plate and foot do not allow for any sideways needle movement. Use these features when your fabric or sewing procedure requires close control, such as edgestitching or making collar points. They are also good for sheers and delicate fabrics, because the small needle hole helps keep fragile fabrics from being drawn into the feed.

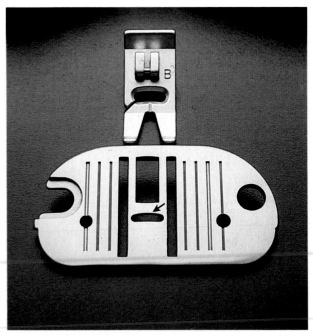

Zigzag plate and foot are the general-purpose plate and foot on a zigzag machine at time of purchase. They are used for zigzag and multi-needle work as well as plain straight stitching on firm fabrics. The needle hole (arrow) in the plate is wider, and the foot has a wider area for the needle to pass through, allowing for side-to-side needle motion. Use this plate and foot for general-purpose sewing.

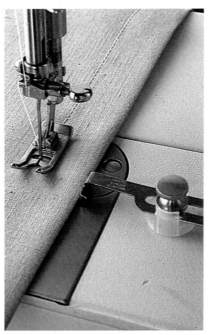

Zipper foot is used to stitch cording, insert zippers, sew bound buttonholes and stitch any seam that has more bulk on one side than the other. It adjusts to either side of the needle.

Seam guide attaches to the machine bed and helps keep seam allowances even. It adjusts to any seam width and swivels for sewing curved seams.

Blindstitch hem foot positions the hem for blindstitch hemming on the machine. This is a fast alternative to hemming by hand.

Even Feed™ foot feeds top and bottom layers together so seams start and end evenly. Use it for vinyl, pile fabrics, bulky knits or other fabrics that tend to stick, slip or stretch. This foot is also useful for topstitching and stitching plaids.

Button foot holds flat buttons in position for attaching with machine zigzag stitch. This foot saves time when sewing several buttons on a garment.

Overedge foot helps keep stitches at full width and prevents curling of flat edges when sewing overedge stitches. Stitches are formed over a hook on the inside edge of the foot.

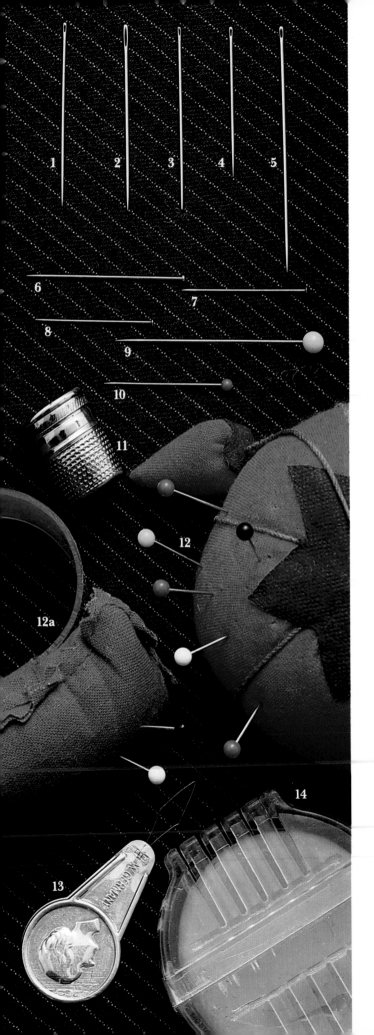

Essential Equipment

Basic sewing is divided into five processes: measuring, cutting, marking, stitching by hand or machine, and pressing. For each of these tasks, there are essential tools to make the steps easier and the results superior. Build an equipment inventory as you add to your sewing skills.

Hand Sewing Equipment

Needles and pins are available in a variety of sizes and styles for different uses. Look for rustproof needles and pins made of brass, nickel-plated steel or stainless steel. Pins with colored ball heads rather than flat heads are easier to see in fabric and less likely to get lost.

1) Sharps are all-purpose, medium length needles used for general sewing.

2) Crewels are generally used for embroidery. They are sharp and of medium length.

3) Ballpoint needles are used on knits. Instead of a sharp point which may pierce the fabric, the rounded end pushes the knit loops apart.

4) Betweens are very short and round-eyed. They help make fine stitches in heavy fabric or quilting.

5) Milliner's needles are long with round eyes, used for making long basting or gathering stitches.

6) Silk pins are used for light to mediumweight fabrics. Size #17 is 1¹⁄₁₆" (2.6 cm) long; #20 is 1¼" (3.2 cm). Both are also available with glass or plastic heads. Extra fine 1¾" (4.5 cm) silk pins are easier to see in fabric because of their length.

7) Straight pins in brass, steel or stainless steel are used for general sewing. They are usually 1¹⁄₁₆" (2.6 cm) long.

8) Pleating pins are only 1" (2.5 cm) long, for pinning delicate fabrics in the seam allowance.

9) Quilting pins are 1¼" (3.2 cm) long, used for heavy materials because of their length.

10) Ballpoint pins are used for knits.

11) Thimble protects your middle finger while hand sewing. It is available in sizes 6 (small) to 12 (large) for individual, snug fit.

12) Pin cushion provides a safe place to store pins. Some pin cushions have an emery pack (an abrasive material) attached for cleaning pins and needles. A wrist pin cushion (**12a**) keeps pins handy.

13) Needle threader eases threading of hand or machine needles.

14) Beeswax with holder strengthens thread and prevents tangling for hand sewing.

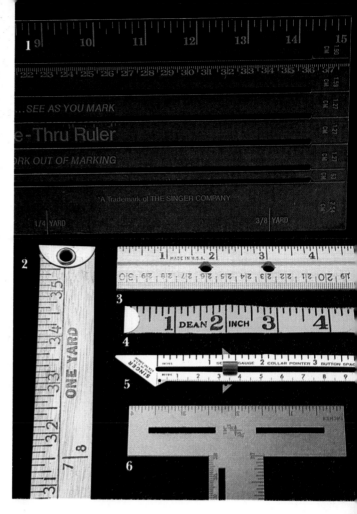

Marking Tools

The symbols on a pattern piece are guides for the accurate construction of the garment. Transferring these symbols from pattern to fabric is essential to fitting and sewing. Because you will be working with several types of fabrics, you will need a variety of marking tools.

1) Tracing wheels come in two types: serrated or smooth edge. The serrated edge makes a dotted line marking. It is suitable for most fabrics but may pierce delicate ones. The smooth-edge tracing wheel protects delicate, smooth fabrics such as silk and chiffon. It makes a solid line marking.

2) Dressmaker's tracing paper is a special waxed carbon paper which transfers the tracing wheel's line to the fabric. Choose a color close to that of the fabric, making sure it can be seen easily.

3) Tailor's chalk or marking pencil marks quickly and easily, directly on the fabric. Chalk rubs off quickly, so use it only when you plan to sew immediately. A tailor tacker **(3a)** holds two pieces of chalk and marks from both sides.

4) Liquid marking pencils make quick work of marking tucks, darts, pleats and pocket locations. One type disappears within 48 hours. The other washes off with water but should not be used on fabrics that show water marks. Pressing may set the marks permanently, so remove marking before pressing the area.

Measuring Tools

Body and pattern measurements both require measuring tools. To ensure a good fit, measure often and accurately with the best tool for the job.

1) See-through ruler lets you see what you measure or mark. This ruler is used to check fabric grainline and to mark buttonholes, tucks and pleats.

2) Yardstick is for general marking and for measuring fabric grainline when laying out the pattern. It should be made of smooth, shellacked hardwood or metal.

3) Ruler is for general marking. The most useful sizes are 12" or 18" (30.5 or 46 cm) long.

4) Tape measure has the flexibility required to take body measurements. Select a 60" (150 cm) long tape with metal tips, made of a material that will not stretch. It should be reversible, with numbers and markings printed on both sides.

5) Seam gauge helps make quick, accurate measurements for hems, buttonholes, scallops and pleats. It is a small, 6" (15 cm) metal or plastic ruler with a sliding marker.

6) See-through T-square is used to locate cross grains, alter patterns and square off straight edges.

17

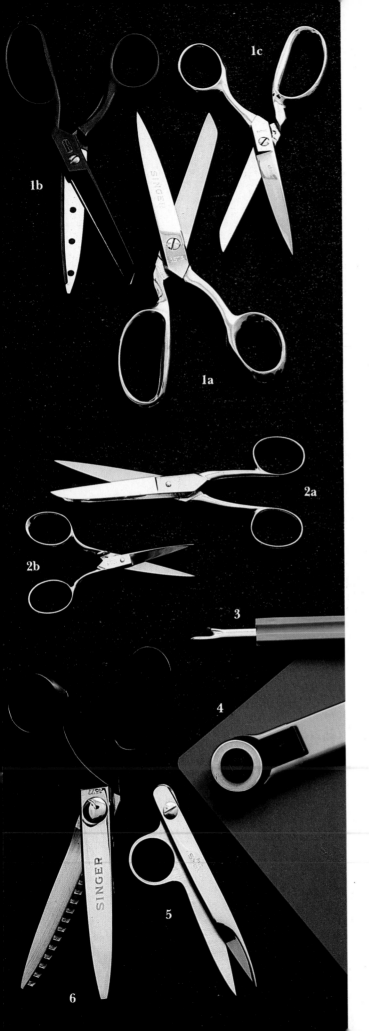

Cutting Tools

Buy quality cutting tools and keep them at their best with periodic sharpening by a qualified professional. Scissors have both handles the same size; shears have one handle larger than the other. The best quality scissors and shears are hot-forged, high-grade steel, honed to a fine cutting edge. Blades should be joined with an adjustable screw (not a rivet) to ensure even pressure along the length of the blade. Sharp shears make clean cuts and well-defined notches. More important, they do not damage fabric. Dull shears slow the cutting process, and make your hand and wrist tire easily. Sewing shears should not be used for other household tasks such as cutting paper or twine. Scissors and shears last longer if you occasionally put a drop of oil on the screw assembly, wipe them clean with a soft dry cloth after use, and store them in a box or pouch.

1) Bent-handled dressmaker's shears are best for pattern cutting because the angle of the lower blade lets fabric lie flat on the cutting surface. Blade lengths of 7" or 8" (18 or 20.5 cm) are most popular, but lengths up to 12" (30.5 cm) are available. Select a blade length appropriate to the size of your hand — shorter lengths for small hands, longer lengths for large hands. Left-handed models are also available. If you sew a great deal, invest in a pair of all-steel, chrome-plated shears (**1a**) for heavy-duty cutting. The lighter models with stainless steel blades and plastic handles (**1b**) are fine for less-frequent sewing or lightweight fabrics. For synthetic fabrics and slippery knits, a serrated-edge shears (**1c**) gives maximum cutting control.

2) Sewing scissors (2a) have one pointed and one rounded tip for trimming and clipping seams and facings. The 6" (15 cm) blade is most practical. Embroidery scissors (**2b**) have 4" or 5" (10 or 12.5 cm) finely-tapered blades. Both points are sharp for use in hand work and precision cutting.

3) Seam ripper quickly rips seams, opens buttonholes and removes stitches. Use carefully to avoid piercing the fabric.

4) Rotary cutter is an adaptation of the giant rotary cutters used by the garment industry. It works like a pizza cutter and can be used by left or right-handed sewers. Use the rotary cutter with a special plastic mat available in different sizes. The mat protects both the cutting surface and the blade. A special locking mechanism retracts the blade for safety.

5) Thread clipper with spring-action blades is more convenient than shears and safer than a seam ripper.

6) Pinking shears or scalloping shears cut a zigzag or scalloped edge instead of a straight one. Used to finish seams and raw edges on many types of fabric, they cut a ravel-resistant edge.

Pressing Tools

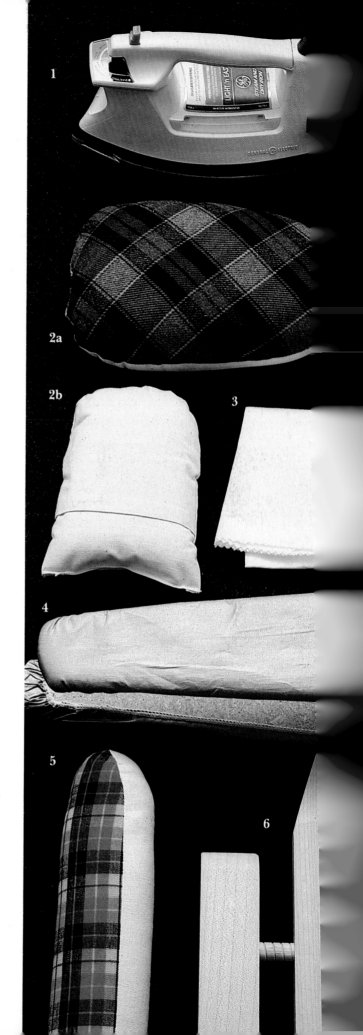

Pressing as you sew is one important procedure that is often neglected. It may seem like a needless interruption, but pressing at each stage of construction is the secret to a perfectly finished garment.

If you need help getting into the pressing habit, locate your pressing equipment near your sewing area. It also helps to press in batches. Do this by stitching as much as possible at the machine. Then press all the stitched areas at one time.

Pressing does not mean ironing. In ironing, you glide the iron over the fabric. In pressing, you move the iron very little while it is in contact with the fabric. Use minimum pressure on the iron, and press in the direction of the fabric grain. Lift the iron to move to another section.

Your pattern directions usually tell when to press, but the general rule is: Press each stitched seam before crossing with another. Press on the wrong side to prevent iron shine, and protect the iron's soleplate by removing pins before pressing.

1) Steam/spray iron should have a wide temperature range to accommodate all fabrics. Buy a dependable, name-brand iron. An iron that steams and sprays at any setting, not just the higher heat settings, is helpful for synthetic fabrics.

2) Tailor's ham or pressing mitt is used when pressing shaped areas such as curved seams, darts, collars or sleeve caps. The ham **(2a)** is a firmly-packed cushion with rounded curves. One side is cotton; the other side is covered with wool to retain more steam. The mitt **(2b)** is similar to the ham but is especially handy for small, hard-to-reach areas. It fits over the hand or a sleeve board.

3) Press cloth helps prevent iron shine and is always used when applying fusible interfacing. The transparent variety allows you to see if the fabric is smooth and the interfacing properly aligned.

4) Sleeve board looks like two small ironing boards attached one on top of the other. It is used when pressing seams and details of small or narrow areas such as sleeves, pants legs or necklines.

5) Seam roll is a firmly-packed cylindrical cushion for pressing seams. The bulk of the fabric falls to the sides and never touches the iron, preventing the seam from making an imprint on the right side of the fabric.

6) Point presser/clapper is made of hardwood and used for pressing seams open in corners and points. The clapper flattens seams by holding steam and heat in the fabric. This tool is used in tailoring to achieve a flat finish and sharp edges on hard-surfaced fabrics.

Special Equipment

Many kinds of special equipment are designed to save time in layout, construction and pressing. The more you sew, the more these aids will become necessities. Just as you would invest in timesaving devices for cooking and cleaning, invest in sewing equipment to make your wardrobe and home decorating projects go faster.

Before using a new product, read all instructions carefully. Learn what special handling or care is required, and what fabrics or techniques it is suited for. Here is an overview of some of these specialized sewing products.

Table-top ironing board is portable and saves space. It is easy to set up near your sewing machine. This ironing board keeps large pieces of fabric on the table so they do not stretch out or drag on the floor. It also helps cultivate the habit of detail pressing while you sew.

Hand steamer is a lightweight steam iron, providing a concentrated area of steam at a low temperature setting. No press cloth is needed, even when pressing on the right side of the fabric. It heats to a steam temperature in less than two minutes and is useful for darts, seams, pleats and hems.

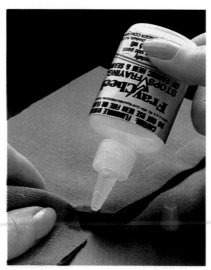

Glue substitutes for pinning or basting by holding fabric, leather, vinyl, felt, trims, patch pockets and zippers in place for permanent stitching. Use it for craft work as well as general sewing. Glue stick is water soluble, so it provides only a temporary bond. Liquid glue can be dotted in seam allowances to hold layers of fabric together.

Liquid ravel preventer is a colorless plastic liquid which prevents fraying by stiffening fabric slightly. It is helpful when you have clipped too far into a seam allowance or want to reinforce a pocket or buttonhole. It darkens light colors slightly, so apply cautiously. The liquid becomes a permanent finish that will withstand laundering and dry cleaning.

Basting tape is double-faced adhesive tape that eliminates pinning and thread basting. Use it on leather and vinyl as well as on fabric. The tape is especially helpful for matching stripes and plaids, applying zippers, and positioning pockets and trims. Do not machine-stitch through the tape, because the adhesive may foul your machine needle.

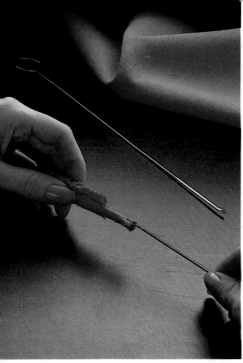

Loop turner is specially designed with a latch hook device at one end to grasp bias tubing or cording and turn it to the right side. It is quicker and easier than attaching a safety pin to one end and working the pin through. Because the wire is so fine, it can be used for very narrow tubing and button loops.

Bodkin threads ribbon, elastic or cord through a casing without twisting. Some bodkins have an eye through which ribbon or elastic is threaded; others have a tweezer or safety pin closure which grabs the elastic. The bodkin above has a ring which slides to tighten the prongs of the pincers.

Point turner pokes out the tailored points in collars, lapels and pockets without risking a tear. Made of wood or plastic, its point fits neatly into corners. Use the point to remove basting thread and the rounded end to hold seamlines open for pressing.

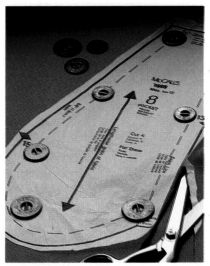

Folding cutting board protects a fine table's finish from pin or shears scratches. It also prevents fabric from slipping while cutting, and holds fabric more securely. Stick pins into it for faster pinning, square off fabric against marked lines, and use the 1" (2.5 cm) squares as an instant measure. The folding feature makes storage easy.

Weights hold a pattern in place for cutting. They eliminate time-consuming pinning and unpinning of the pattern and protect fabrics that would be permanently marked by pins. Weights are most easily used on smaller pattern pieces. Some sewers use items like cans of vegetables in place of retail weights.

Magnetic pin catcher and pin cushion keep all-steel pins in their place. The pin catcher attaches to the throat plate of the machine to catch pins as you pull them out while stitching. The magnetic, weighted pin cushion is more convenient than an ordinary one, and is especially handy for picking pins off the floor.

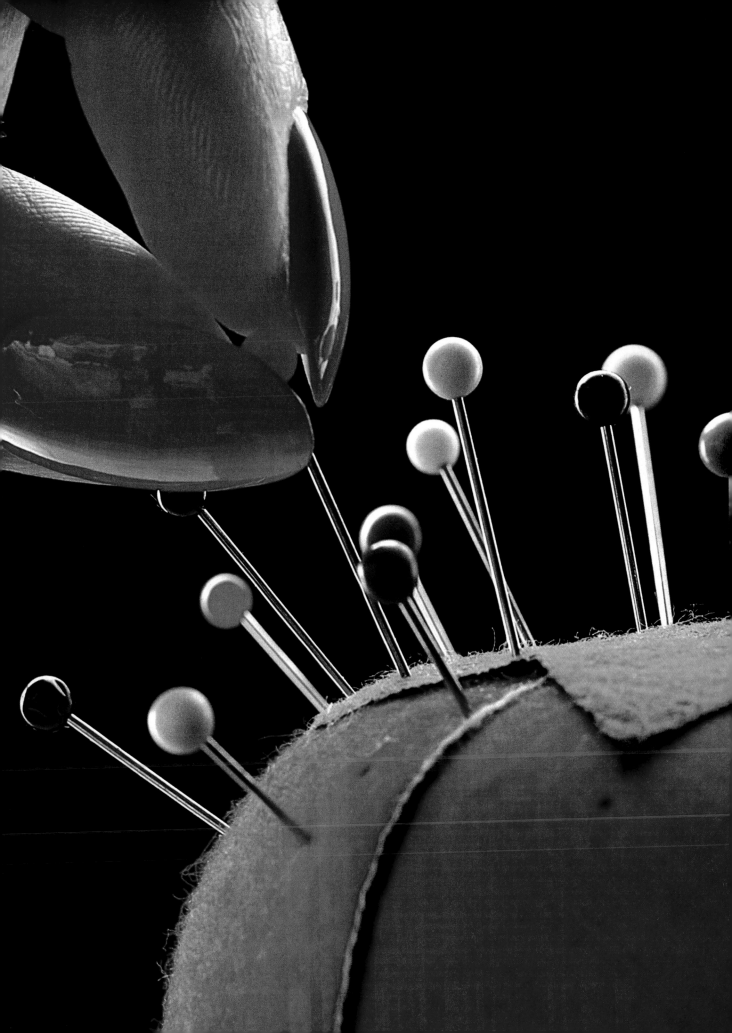

Getting Started

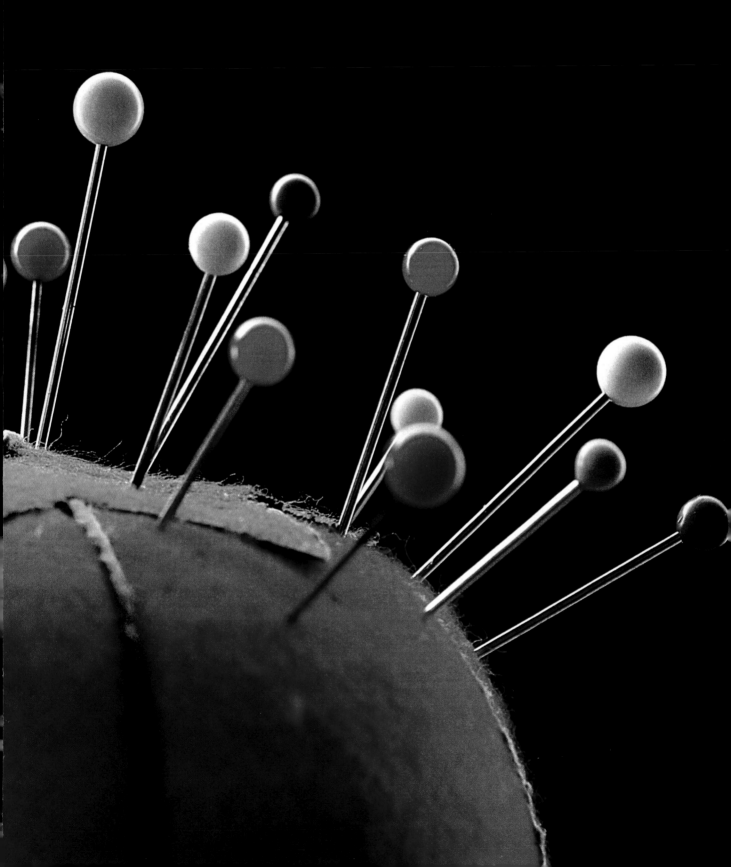

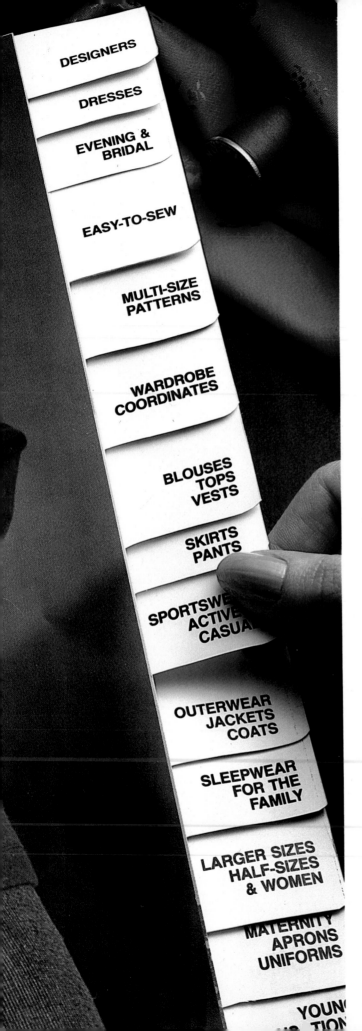

DESIGNERS

DRESSES

EVENING & BRIDAL

EASY-TO-SEW

MULTI-SIZE PATTERNS

WARDROBE COORDINATES

BLOUSES TOPS VESTS

SKIRTS PANTS

SPORTSWE ACTIVE CASUA

OUTERWEAR JACKETS COATS

SLEEPWEAR FOR THE FAMILY

LARGER SIZES HALF-SIZES & WOMEN

MATERNITY APRONS UNIFORMS

YOUN

The Pattern

Shopping a pattern catalog is more creative than shopping a ready-to-wear catalog. In a pattern catalog, you aren't limited to the fabric, color, skirt length or buttons you see on the pages. You are the designer of your own fashion. You can choose the combination that flatters you and expresses your own personal style.

Pattern selection has never been better. Designer styles are available in the same season that they appear in ready-to-wear. There are easy patterns for the sewer with limited time. You will find patterns for accessories, home decoration, evening wear, men's and boys' fashions, and almost every kind of women's or children's garment.

The pattern catalog is divided into categories by size or fashion look, marked by index tabs. The newest fashions usually appear in the first few pages of each category. Pattern illustrations are accompanied by information on recommended fabrics and yardage requirements. An index at the back of the catalog lists patterns in numerical order along with their page numbers. The back of the catalog also includes a complete size chart for every figure type: male, female, children and infants.

Match the pattern's level of sewing difficulty to your sewing experience. For success, select a pattern appropriate to your sewing skill. If your time or patience is limited, stay with simpler styles.

The number of pattern pieces listed on the back of the pattern is a clue to the complexity of the pattern. The fewer the pieces, the easier the pattern. Details like shirt cuffs, collar bands, pleats and tucks also make a pattern more difficult to sew. Easy-to-sew patterns feature few of these details.

All pattern companies follow a uniform sizing based on standard body measurements. This is not exactly the same as ready-to-wear sizing. To select the right pattern size, first take your standard body measurements. Wear your usual undergarments and use a tape measure that doesn't stretch. For accuracy, have another person measure you. Record your measurements and compare them with the size chart on page 27.

How to Take Standard Body Measurements

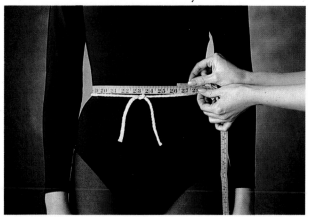

1) Waistline. Tie a string or piece of elastic around your middle and allow it to roll to your natural waistline. Measure at this exact location with tape measure. Leave string in place as a reference for measuring hips and back waist length.

2) Hips. Measure around the fullest part. This is usually 7" to 9" (18 to 23 cm) below the waistline, depending on your height.

3) High bust. Place tape measure under arms, across widest part of back and above full bustline. Pattern size charts do not include a high bust measurement, but this measurement should be compared with the full bust to choose the right size pattern.

4) Full bust. Place tape measure under arms, across widest part of the back and fullest part of bustline. Note: If there is a difference of 2" (5 cm) or more between high and full bust, select pattern size by high bust measurement.

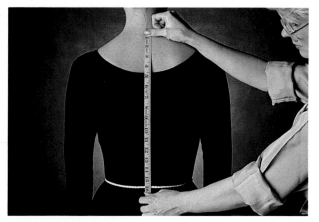

5) Back waist length. Measure from middle of the most prominent bone at the base of the neck down to waistline string.

6) Height. Measure without shoes. Stand with your back against a wall. Place a ruler on top of your head and mark the wall. Measure from the mark to the floor.

Female Figure Types

Young Junior Teen
About 5'1" to 5'3" (1.55 to 1.60 m) tall. Developing teen or preteen figure, with small, high bust. Waistline is larger in proportion to bust.

Junior Petite
About 5' to 5'1" (1.53 to 1.55 m) tall. Well-developed, shorter figure, with smaller body build and shorter back waist length than a Junior.

Junior
About 5'4" to 5'5" (1.63 to 1.65 m) tall. Well-developed figure, slightly shorter in height and back waist length than a Miss.

Miss Petite
About 5'2" to 5'4" (1.57 to 1.63 m) tall. Well-developed and well-proportioned shorter figure, with a shorter back waist length and slightly larger waist than a Miss.

Miss
About 5'5" to 5'6" (1.65 to 1.68 m) tall. Well-developed and well-proportioned in all areas. Considered the average figure.

Half-size
About 5'2" to 5'3" (1.57 to 1.60 m) tall. Fully-developed but shorter than the Miss. Shoulders are narrower than a Miss Petite. Waist is larger in proportion to bust than a Woman.

Woman
About 5'5" to 5'6" (1.65 to 1.68 m) tall. Same height as Miss, but larger and more fully mature, making all other measurements proportionately larger.

Maternity
Corresponds to Miss sizes. Measurements are for a figure five months pregnant, but patterns are designed to provide ease through the ninth month.

Female Figure Size Chart

To choose the right size pattern, take your measurements as directed on page 25. Then determine your figure type using the descriptions on the opposite page. Find your figure type on the chart below. Locate the column of numbers that most closely matches your measurements. Choose dress, blouse and suit patterns by bust size; pants and skirt patterns by hip size.

Inches

Young Junior/Teen:

Size	5/6	7/8	9/10	11/12	13/14	15/16
Bust	28	29	30½	32	33½	35
Waist	22	23	24	25	26	27
Hip	31	32	33½	35	36½	38
Back Waist Length	13½	14	14½	15	15⅜	15¾

Junior Petite:

Size	3jp	5jp	7jp	9jp	11jp	13jp
Bust	30	31	32	33	34	35
Waist	22	23	24	25	26	27
Hip	31	32	33	34	35	36
Back Waist Length	14	14¼	14½	14¾	15	15¼

Junior:

Size	5	7	9	11	13	15
Bust	30	31	32	33½	35	37
Waist	22½	23½	24½	25½	27	29
Hip	32	33	34	35½	37	39
Back Waist Length	15	15¼	15½	15¾	16	16¼

Miss Petite:

Size	6mp	8mp	10mp	12mp	14mp	16mp
Bust	30½	31½	32½	34	36	38
Waist	23½	24½	25½	27	28½	30½
Hip	32½	33½	34½	36	38	40
Back Waist Length	14½	14¾	15	15¼	15½	15¾

Miss:

Size	6	8	10	12	14	16	18	20
Bust	30½	31½	32½	34	36	38	40	42
Waist	23	24	25	26½	28	30	32	34
Hip	32½	33½	34½	36	38	40	42	44
Back Waist Length	15½	15¾	16	16¼	16½	16¾	17	17¼

Half-size:

Size	10½	12½	14½	16½	18½	20½	22½	24½
Bust	33	35	37	39	41	43	45	47
Waist	27	29	31	33	35	37½	40	42½
Hip	35	37	39	41	43	45½	48	50½
Back Waist Length	15	15¼	15½	15¾	15⅞	16	16⅛	16¼

Woman:

Size	38	40	42	44	46	48	50	52
Bust	42	44	46	48	50	52	54	56
Waist	35	37	39	41½	44	46½	49	51½
Hip	44	46	48	50	52	54	56	58
Back Waist Length	17¼	17⅜	17½	17⅝	17¾	17⅞	18	18⅛

Maternity:

Size	6	8	10	12	14	16
Bust	34	35	36	37½	39½	41½
Waist	28½	29½	30½	32	33½	35½
Hip	35½	36½	37½	39	41	43
Back Waist Length	15½	15¾	16	16¼	16½	16¾

Centimeters

Young Junior/Teen:

Size	5/6	7/8	9/10	11/12	13/14	15/16
Bust	71	74	78	81	85	89
Waist	56	58	61	64	66	69
Hip	79	81	85	89	93	97
Back Waist Length	34.5	35.5	37	38	39	40

Junior Petite:

Size	3jp	5jp	7jp	9jp	11jp	13jp
Bust	76	79	81	84	87	89
Waist	56	58	61	64	66	69
Hip	79	81	84	87	89	92
Back Waist Length	35.5	36	37	37.5	38	39

Junior:

Size	5	7	9	11	13	15
Bust	76	79	81	85	89	94
Waist	57	60	62	65	69	74
Hip	81	84	87	90	94	99
Back Waist Length	38	39	39.5	40	40.5	41.5

Miss Petite:

Size	6mp	8mp	10mp	12mp	14mp	16mp
Bust	78	80	83	87	92	97
Waist	60	62	65	69	73	78
Hip	83	85	88	92	97	102
Back Waist Length	37	37.5	38	39	39.5	40

Miss:

Size	6	8	10	12	14	16	18	20
Bust	78	80	83	87	92	97	102	107
Waist	58	61	64	67	71	76	81	87
Hip	83	85	88	92	97	102	107	112
Back Waist Length	39.5	40	40.5	41.5	42	42.5	43	44

Half-size:

Size	10½	12½	14½	16½	18½	20½	22½	24½
Bust	84	89	94	99	104	109	114	119
Waist	69	74	79	84	89	96	102	108
Hip	89	94	99	104	109	116	122	128
Back Waist Length	38	39	39.5	40	40.5	40.5	41	41.5

Woman:

Size	38	40	42	44	46	48	50	52
Bust	107	112	117	122	127	132	137	142
Waist	89	94	99	105	112	118	124	131
Hip	112	117	122	127	132	137	142	147
Back Waist Length	44	44	44.5	45	45	45.5	46	46

Maternity:

Size	6	8	10	12	14	16
Bust	87	89	92	95	100	105
Waist	72	75	77.5	81	85	90
Hip	90	93	95	99	104	109
Back Waist Length	39.5	40	40.5	41.5	42	42.5

The Pattern Envelope

The pattern envelope contains a wealth of information, from a description of the garment to the amount of fabric needed. It gives ideas for fabric and color selection. The envelope helps you determine the degree of sewing difficulty with labels that indicate whether the style is a designer original, easy-to-sew or only suitable for certain fabrics. On the pattern envelope, you'll also find all the information needed to select fabric and notions.

The Envelope Front

Size and figure type are indicated at the top or side of the pattern. If the pattern is multi-sized, such as 8-10-12, you will find cutting lines for all three sizes on one pattern.

Pattern company name and style number are prominently displayed at the top or along the side of the pattern envelope.

Designer original patterns, indicated by the designer's name, often contain more difficult-to-sew details such as tucks, topstitching, linings or underlinings. For sewers who have the time and skill, these patterns provide designer fashions that duplicate ready-to-wear.

SIZE 10 / MISS

6157

$4.00 U.S.A.

PATTERN

Designer

BONUS—Pattern includes special chart on how to work with plaids.

Views are alternate designs of the pattern. They may show optional trims, lengths, fabric combinations or design details to appeal to a beginner, or challenge an experienced sewer.

Labels may identify a pattern that has easy construction methods, is designed for timesaving sewing, has special fitting or size-related information, or shows how to handle special fabrics like plaids, knits or lace. Each pattern company has special categories and names for these designs.

Fashion illustration or photograph shows the main pattern design. It suggests suitable fabric types such as wool or cotton, and fabric designs such as print or plaid. If you are unsure of your fabric choice, use the pattern illustration as your guide. It is the designer's interpretation of the fashion.

The Envelope Back

Back views show the details and style of the back of the garments.

Number of pattern pieces gives an idea of how easy or complicated the pattern is to sew.

Style number is repeated on the back of the envelope.

Garment descriptions include style, fit and construction information.

Fabric types suitable for the garments are suggested. Use them as a general guide to fabric selection. The special advice, such as "unsuitable for stripes or obvious diagonals," alerts you to fabrics that are not appropriate.

Body measurement and size chart is a reference to determine if you need to make alterations. For a multi-sized pattern, compare your measurements with those in the chart to decide which cutting line to use.

Metric equivalents of body measurements and yardage are included for countries which use the metric system.

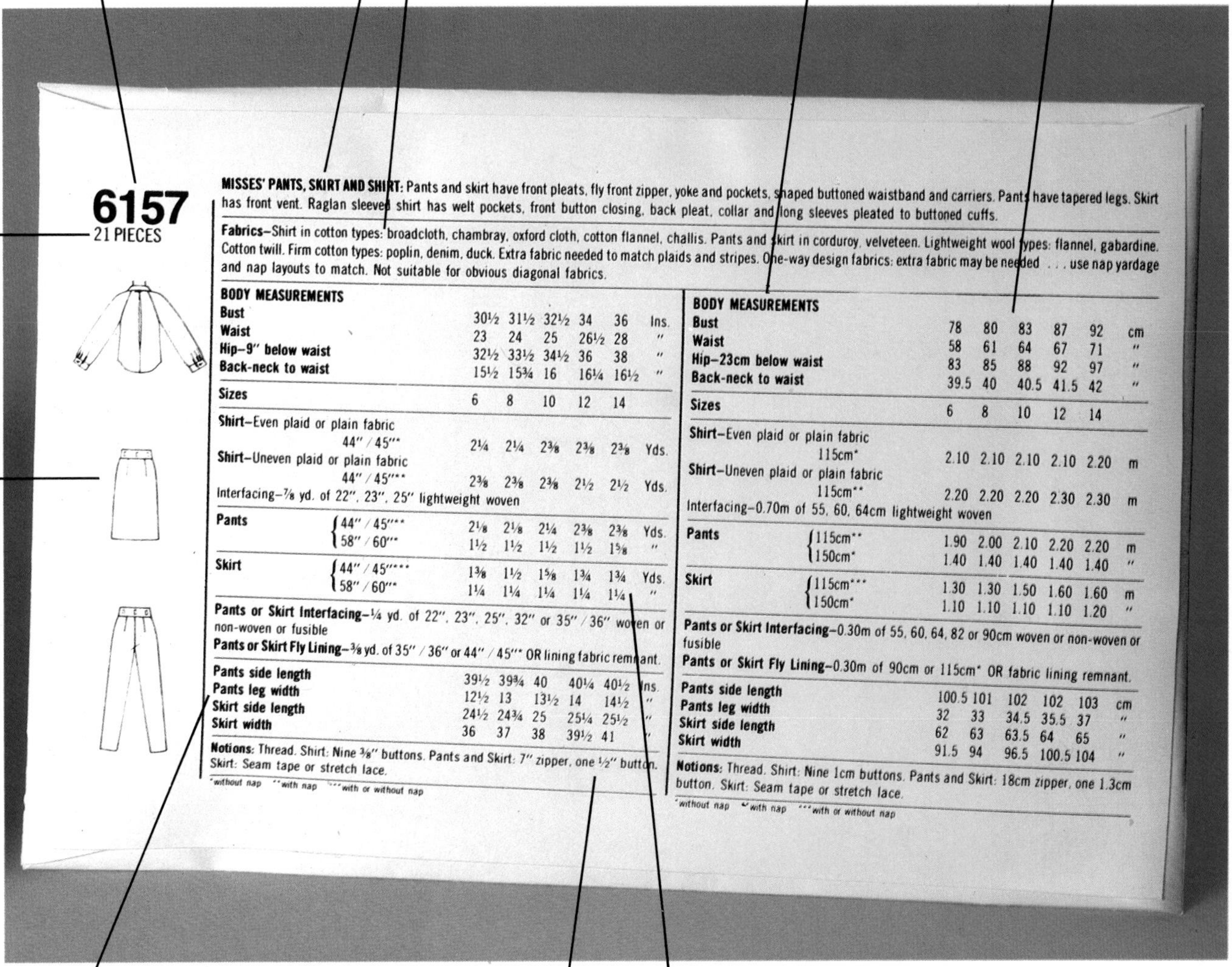

6157
21 PIECES

MISSES' PANTS, SKIRT AND SHIRT: Pants and skirt have front pleats, fly front zipper, yoke and pockets, shaped buttoned waistband and carriers. Pants have tapered legs. Skirt has front vent. Raglan sleeved shirt has welt pockets, front button closing, back pleat, collar and long sleeves pleated to buttoned cuffs.

Fabrics—Shirt in cotton types: broadcloth, chambray, oxford cloth, cotton flannel, challis. Pants and skirt in corduroy, velveteen. Lightweight wool types: flannel, gabardine. Cotton twill. Firm cotton types: poplin, denim, duck. Extra fabric needed to match plaids and stripes. One-way design fabrics: extra fabric may be needed . . . use nap yardage and nap layouts to match. Not suitable for obvious diagonal fabrics.

BODY MEASUREMENTS

Bust	30½	31½	32½	34	36	Ins.
Waist	23	24	25	26½	28	"
Hip—9" below waist	32½	33½	34½	36	38	"
Back-neck to waist	15½	15¾	16	16¼	16½	"
Sizes	6	8	10	12	14	
Shirt—Even plaid or plain fabric 44"/45"*	2¼	2¼	2⅜	2⅜	2⅜	Yds.
Shirt—Uneven plaid or plain fabric 44"/45"**	2⅜	2⅜	2⅜	2½	2½	Yds.
Interfacing—⅞ yd. of 22", 23", 25" lightweight woven						
Pants {44"/45"**	2⅛	2⅛	2¼	2⅜	2⅜	Yds.
{58"/60"*	1½	1½	1½	1½	1⅝	"
Skirt {44"/45"***	1⅜	1½	1⅝	1¾	1¾	Yds.
{58"/60"**	1¼	1¼	1¼	1¼	1¼	"
Pants or Skirt Interfacing—¼ yd. of 22", 23", 25", 32" or 35"/36" woven or non-woven or fusible						
Pants or Skirt Fly Lining—⅜ yd. of 35"/36" or 44"/45"* OR lining fabric remnant.						
Pants side length	39½	39¾	40	40¼	40½	Ins.
Pants leg width	12½	13	13½	14	14½	"
Skirt side length	24½	24¾	25	25¼	25½	"
Skirt width	36	37	38	39½	41	"

Notions: Thread. Shirt: Nine ⅜" buttons. Pants and Skirt: 7" zipper, one ½" button. Skirt: Seam tape or stretch lace.

*without nap   **with nap   ***with or without nap

BODY MEASUREMENTS

Bust	78	80	83	87	92	cm
Waist	58	61	64	67	71	"
Hip—23cm below waist	83	85	88	92	97	"
Back-neck to waist	39.5	40	40.5	41.5	42	"
Sizes	6	8	10	12	14	
Shirt—Even plaid or plain fabric 115cm*	2.10	2.10	2.10	2.10	2.20	m
Shirt—Uneven plaid or plain fabric 115cm**	2.20	2.20	2.20	2.30	2.30	m
Interfacing—0.70m of 55, 60, 64cm lightweight woven						
Pants {115cm**	1.90	2.00	2.10	2.20	2.20	m
{150cm*	1.40	1.40	1.40	1.40	1.40	"
Skirt {115cm***	1.30	1.30	1.50	1.60	1.60	m
{150cm**	1.10	1.10	1.10	1.10	1.20	"
Pants or Skirt Interfacing—0.30m of 55, 60, 64, 82 or 90cm woven or non-woven or fusible						
Pants or Skirt Fly Lining—0.30m of 90cm or 115cm* OR fabric lining remnant.						
Pants side length	100.5	101	102	102	103	cm
Pants leg width	32	33	34.5	35.5	37	"
Skirt side length	62	63	63.5	64	65	"
Skirt width	91.5	94	96.5	100.5	104	"

Notions: Thread. Shirt: Nine 1cm buttons. Pants and Skirt: 18cm zipper, one 1.3cm button. Skirt: Seam tape or stretch lace.

*without nap   **with nap   ***with or without nap

Finished garment measurements indicate finished length and width. You may need to make length adjustments. The "width at lower edge" is the measurement at the hemmed edge, indicating the fullness of the garment.

Notions, such as thread, zipper, buttons and seam binding, which are required for garment construction are listed. Purchase them at the same time as the fabric to ensure a good color match.

Yardage block tells you how much fabric to buy for the size and garment view you have selected. Yardage for lining, interfacing and trims is also listed. To determine how much fabric you need, match the garment or view and the fabric width at the left with your size at the top of the chart. The number where the two columns meet is the number of yards to buy. The most common fabric widths are given. If the width of your fabric is not given, check the conversion chart at the back of the pattern catalog. Some patterns list the extra yardage required for napped fabrics or uneven plaids.

Inside the Pattern

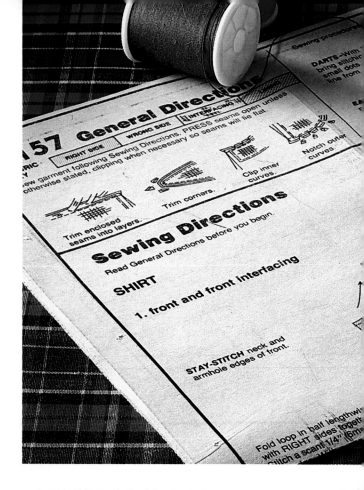

Open the pattern envelope to find the printed pattern pieces and the direction sheet which guides you, step-by-step, through the construction of the garment. Read through the direction sheet *before* cutting or sewing. Use it to plan and organize your sewing time, and alert you to the techniques you need to know as you progress.

Views of a single garment are labeled by number or letter. Patterns which include several different garments such as a skirt, jacket and pants (called *wardrobe patterns*) usually feature only one version of each. In this case, each garment is identified by name only. All pattern pieces are identified with a number and name, such as *skirt front.*

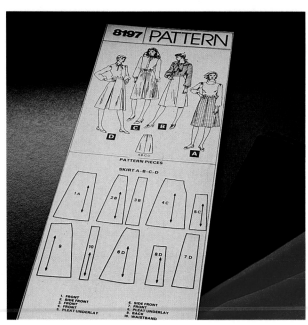

Fashion drawings and views are featured prominently on the direction sheet, sketched as they appear on the front of the envelope or as detailed line drawings. Some patterns illustrate each garment separately with the pattern pieces used in its construction. Most patterns illustrate all the pattern pieces together, with a key to identify the pieces used for each garment or view.

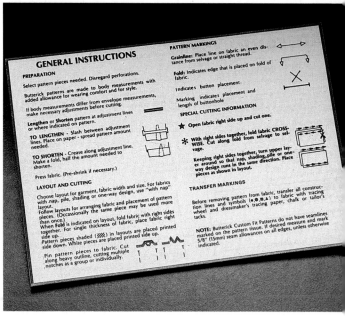

General instructions are given as a short refresher sewing course. These instructions may have a different name on each company's pattern, but they generally contain tips on how to use the pattern. Included is information on pattern and fabric preparation; explanation of pattern markings; cutting, layout and marking tips; and a short glossary of sewing terms. The easy-to-sew and beginner patterns often incorporate these tips into the step-by-step instructions.

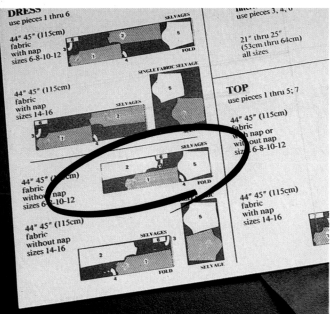

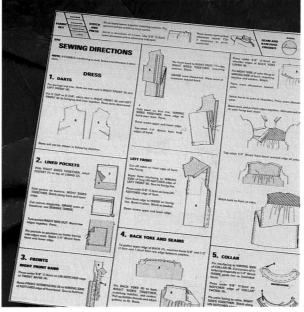

Cutting layouts are shown for each garment view. They differ according to the width of the fabric, pattern size and whether the fabric is with or without nap. Layouts for interfacing and lining are also included. When the fabric is to be cut in a single thickness or on the crosswise grain, the pattern layout indicates this with a symbol, explained in the general instructions. A pattern piece, right side up, is illustrated without shading; wrong side up, it is shaded or scored. Circle the layout for the correct pattern size, fabric width and view.

Sewing directions are a step-by-step guide to constructing the garment, arranged by views. Beside each instruction is a sketch illustrating the sewing technique. The right side of the fabric usually appears shaded; the wrong side, plain. Interfacing is indicated with dots. Together, the sketch and the directions give you a clear picture of exactly what to do. Remember that these are only general directions. An alternative technique may be more effective for the fabric you are using.

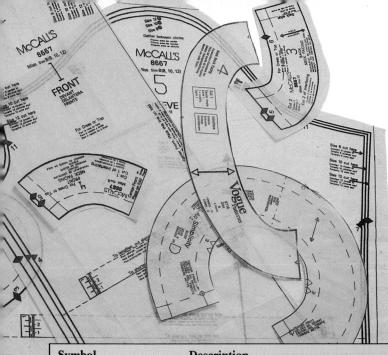

The Pattern Pieces

The pattern piece tissue may look like it is printed with secret symbols but, like international road signs, these markings are universal symbols used by all pattern companies. Pattern symbols are used from the time you start to lay out the pattern until you finish the hem or sew the last button in place.

Pattern pieces have instructions as well as symbols printed on them. Follow these instructions just as carefully as you follow those on the direction sheet.

Layout and cutting symbols such as grainlines do not need to be transferred to the fabric. Construction symbols must be transferred to the fabric for accurate garment construction (pages 51 to 53).

Symbol	Description	How to Use
	Grainline. Heavy solid line with arrows at each end.	Place pattern piece on fabric with arrow parallel to selvage.
	Fold Bracket. Long bracket with arrows at each end or "place on fold" instruction.	Place pattern piece with arrows or edge exactly on fold of fabric.
	Cutting line. Heavy solid line along outer edge of pattern. May also designate a "cut-off" line for a certain view.	Cut on this line. When more than one size is printed on one piece, use the cutting line for size that fits best.
	Adjustment line. Double line indicating where pattern can be lengthened or shortened before cutting.	To shorten, make a tuck in pattern between lines. To lengthen, cut pattern between lines and spread apart.
	Notches. Diamond shapes along cutting line, used for matching seams. Numbered in order in which seams are joined.	Cut out into margin of pattern or make short snips into seam allowance. Match like-numbered notches accurately.
	Seamline. Long, broken line, usually ⅝" (1.5 cm) inside cutting line. Multi-sized patterns do not have printed seamlines.	Unless otherwise specified, stitch ⅝" (1.5 cm) from cut edge.
	Foldline. Solid line marking where garment is to be folded during construction.	Fold along this line when sewing facings, hems, tucks or pleats.
	Dart. Broken line and dots forming a "V" shape, usually at hipline, bustline or elbow.	Mark, fold along center line and carefully match lines and dots. Stitch to a point.
	Dots (large and small), squares or triangles. Usually found along seamlines or darts.	Areas of construction where precise matching, clipping or stitching is essential.
	Easing line. Short, broken line with small dot at each end, marking area to be eased.	Easestitch larger piece; pull up stitching to match smaller piece.
	Gathering lines. Two solid or broken lines, or small dots at each end, marking an area to be gathered.	Make two rows of easestitching between dots of larger piece; pull up stitching so dots match with those on smaller piece.
	Hemline. Hem allowance is printed on the cutting line.	Turn hem up the specified amount, adjusting as necessary.
	Zipper placement. Parallel rows of triangles along seamline where zipper is to be inserted.	Insert zipper so pull tab and bottom stop are positioned where indicated.
	Detail positions. Broken lines indicating placement of pockets, tucks or other details.	Mark and position detail where indicated.
	Button and buttonhole placements. Solid lines indicate length of buttonhole; "X" or illustration shows button size and placement.	Mark and position where indicated.

Adjusting the Pattern Length

Depending on your measurements, you may need to shorten or lengthen pattern pieces such as the bodice or sleeve of a blouse or dress, or the hipline of a skirt or pants. Make these alterations in the pattern before cutting, using the adjustment lines marked on the pattern pieces. Some patterns may also indicate a line for folding a tuck to shorten the pattern to convert from one figure type to another. For example, a Miss pattern may also be sized for a Miss Petite figure. New dart positions are also indicated on the pattern. If there are no adjustment lines, the piece can usually be lengthened or shortened at the bottom.

To determine whether length adjustments are necessary, first press the pattern pieces with a dry iron to smooth out wrinkles. Measure the bodice front and back pieces from seamline of shoulder to seamline of waistline, not from cutting edge to cutting edge. Compare this with your own shoulder-to-waistline measurement in front and back. The pattern piece must be at least ½" to ¾" (1.3 to 2 cm) longer than your body measurement to allow sufficient ease.

Measure the skirt front and back pieces from waistline seamline to hemline. Compare with your body measurements and the hem length you want. Shorten or lengthen the pattern as needed along the adjustment lines.

How to Shorten the Pattern

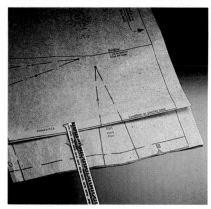

1) Fold the pattern between adjustment lines. Fold a tuck, half the amount to be shortened. Total amount shortened is twice the depth of the tuck.

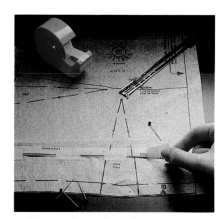

2) Pin tuck in place. Measure length of pattern piece with tape measure or ruler for accuracy. Tape fold in place. Remove pins.

3) Draw new cutting line on pattern if necessary. Be sure to keep grainline straight. Make dart adjustments if necessary.

How to Lengthen the Pattern

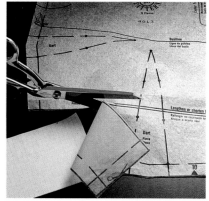

1) Cut the pattern apart along adjustment line. Place graph or tissue paper underneath.

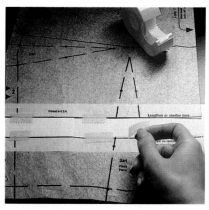

2) Spread the cut pattern edges apart the amount to be lengthened. Tape pattern pieces in place, keeping grainline straight.

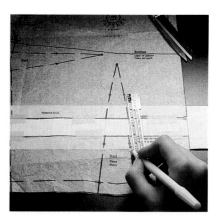

3) Draw new cutting and marking lines. Trim away excess paper. Check dart placement, and adjust point of darts if necessary.

Fabric Essentials

All fabrics are based on two kinds of fibers: *natural* or *man-made*. Natural fibers are those derived from plants or animals: cotton, wool, silk and linen. Man-made fibers are produced by chemical processes. They include polyester, nylon, acetate, spandex and many others.

Combining natural and man-made fibers produces *blends* which give you the best qualities of several fibers. For example, the strength of nylon may be added to the warmth of wool, the easy care of polyester to the comfort of cotton.

There is an almost endless variety of blends available, and each one behaves differently. Check the fiber content on the bolt end for the kinds and quantities of fibers used. Care instructions are also listed. Examine the *hand* of the fabric — how it feels, how it drapes, whether it crushes easily or ravels, whether it stretches. Drape the fabric over your hand or arm to determine if it is as soft or crisp, heavy or light, as you need for a particular project.

Fabrics are also classified by *fabrication,* meaning how they are made. All fabrics are either *woven, knit* or *nonwoven.* The most common woven is the plain weave construction. This is found in fabrics like muslins, poplin and taffeta. Denim and gabardine are diagonal weaves. Cotton sateen is a satin weave. Knits also have several classifications. Jersey is an example of a plain knit. Sweater knits can be made by the purl, patterned or raschel knit processes. Felt is an example of a nonwoven fabric.

Selecting the right fabric for your sewing project takes a little practice. Refer to the back of the pattern envelope for suggestions, and learn to feel the hand of fabric. Quality fabric doesn't have to be expensive. Choose well-made fabric that will wear well and stay looking good.

Easy-to-Sew Fabrics

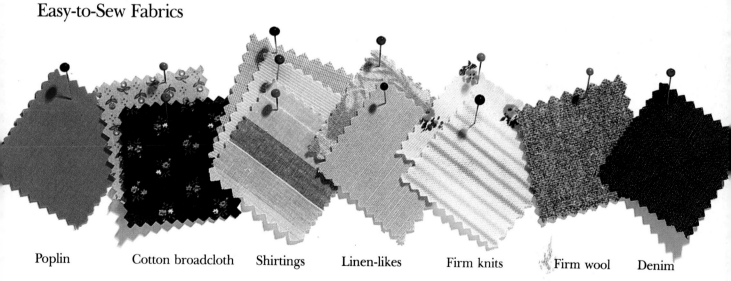

Poplin   Cotton broadcloth   Shirtings   Linen-likes   Firm knits   Firm wool   Denim

There are many fabrics that are easy and quick to sew. These fabrics are generally plain weave or firm knit, of medium weight. Most do not require complicated seam finishes or special handling, since they ravel little or not at all.

Small prints, overall prints and narrow stripes are easy to sew because they do not require matching at the seams. Prints, especially if they are dark, can hide stitching imperfections.

Plain weave fabrics like poplin or cotton broadcloth are always good choices. Stable or moderate-stretch knits do not need seam finishing, and their stretchability makes fitting easier. Natural fiber fabrics, such as cottons and lightweight wools, are easy to sew because stitching easily blends into these fabrics.

For more examples of easy-to-sew fabrics, consult the suggested fabrics that are listed on the backs of easy-to-sew patterns.

Handling Special Fabrics

Certain fabrics, because of their design or fabrication, need special attention during layout and construction. Some easy-to-sew fabrics fall into this category. The special handling required is usually not difficult. Often you need only add one more step, such as a seam finish, or exercise a little more care.

1) Napped and pile fabrics like velvet, velveteen, velour, flannel and corduroy require special care in cutting out. These fabrics appear light and shiny when brushed in one lengthwise direction, and dark when brushed in the other direction. To prevent your garment from having a two-toned look, you must follow the "with nap" layouts on the pattern instruction sheet. Decide which way you want the nap to lie, and cut all pattern pieces with the top edges facing the same direction.

Although satin and moiré taffeta are not napped fabrics, their shiny surfaces reflect light differently in each lengthwise direction. Decide which effect you prefer, and use a one-way layout.

2) Sheer fabrics look best with special seams and seam finishes. Unfinished seam allowances detract from the fragile, see-through look of voile, batiste, eyelet or chiffon. French seams are a classic choice, but other seam finishes can also be used.

3) Twill weave fabrics like denim and gabardine have diagonal ridges. If these ridges are very noticeable, use a "with nap" layout for cutting, and avoid patterns that are not suitable for obvious diagonals. Denim ravels easily and requires enclosed seams.

4) Plaids and stripes require special care in layout and cutting (pages 46 to 49). To match plaids and large stripes at seams, you need to buy extra fabric. Buy ¼ to ½ yard (.25 to .50 m) more than the pattern calls for, depending on the size of the design.

5) Knits must be handled gently during construction to keep them from stretching out of shape. Special stitches and seam finishes (pages 78 and 79) are needed to maintain the right amount of stretch.

6) One-way design fabrics, such as some flower and paisley prints, require a "with nap" cutting layout so the design does not go up one side of the garment and down the other. Border prints are cut on the crosswise rather than lengthwise grain of the fabric. They usually require more yardage. Select patterns which show a border print view and specify the correct yardage.

Guide to Fabrics and Sewing Techniques

Type	Fabric	Plain Seam or Edge Finish	Seam	Machine Needle Size	Thread Type & Weight
Sheer to lightweight	Gauze, voile, chiffon, organza, crepe de chine, fine lace, tulle, net, georgette	Stitched and pinked, zigzag	French, mock French, self-bound, double-stitched	9/65	Extra fine: silk, mercerized cotton, or cotton/polyester
Lightweight	Silk, shirtings, gingham, broadcloth, oxford cloth, calico, lightweight linens, chambray, seersucker, tricot, eyelet, challis, organdy, muslin, batiste, dimity, lawn, piqué	Stitched and pinked, zigzag, selvage	French, mock French, self-bound	11/75	Extra fine: silk or mercerized cotton; all-purpose: cotton/polyester
Light to mediumweight knits	Cotton knits, tricot, cotton/polyester knits, jersey knits, light sweater knits, stretch terry, stretch velour	Zigzag, straight with overedge	Double-stitched, straight and zigzag, narrow zigzag, straight stretch, elastic stretch	14/90 Ballpoint	All-purpose: cotton/polyester or long-fiber polyester
Mediumweight	Cotton, wool, wool flannel, rayon, linen and linen types, chintz, wool crepe, gabardine, chino, poplin, denim, corduroy, velvet, velveteen, velour, taffeta, satin, double knits, sweatshirt knits	Stitched and pinked, zigzag, selvage, turned and stitched, bound finishes	Welt, lapped, flat-fell, mock flat-fell	14/90 (Ballpoint for knits)	All-purpose: cotton/polyester, long-fiber polyester or mercerized cotton
Mediumweight/ suiting weight	Wool, wool blends, tweeds, flannels, gabardine, twill, mohair, boucle, heavy poplin, heavy denim, double knits, quilted fabric	Stitched and pinked, zigzag, selvage, bound finishes	Welt, lapped, flat-fell, mock flat-fell	14/90 16/100	All-purpose: cotton/polyester or mercerized cotton
Medium to heavyweight	Wool, wool blends, heavy wool flannel, fake fur, fleece, canvas, heavy cotton duck, coating, sailcloth, upholstery fabric	Stitched and pinked, selvage	Welt, lapped, mock flat-fell	16/100 18/110	Heavy-duty: cotton or cotton/polyester; topstitching and buttonhole twist
No grain (nonwoven)	Leather, suede, reptile (natural and man-made), buckskin, calfskin, plastic, felt		Welt, lapped, mock flat-fell	14/90 16/100 Wedge-point	All-purpose or heavy-duty (all types)

Interfacing

Interfacing plays a supporting role in almost every garment. It is the inner layer of fabric used to shape and support details like collars, cuffs, waistbands, pockets, lapels and buttonholes. Even simple styles often need interfacing to add stability to necklines, facings or hems. Interfacing adds body to garments and helps keep them crisp through repeated washings and wearings.

Interfacings come in many different fibers and weights. The pattern may require more than one kind. Choose interfacing according to the weight of the fashion fabric, the kind of shaping required and the way the garment will be cleaned. Generally, interfacing should be the same weight or lighter than the fashion fabric. Drape two layers of the fabric and the interfacing together to see if they hang well. Areas like collars and cuffs usually need stiffer interfacing. For sheer fabrics, another piece of the fashion fabric may be the best interfacing.

Interfacings are available in *woven* or *nonwoven* fabrics. Woven interfacing has a lengthwise and crosswise grain. It must be cut with the same grain as the part of the garment to be interfaced. Nonwoven interfacing is made by bonding fibers together; it has no grain. Stable nonwovens can be cut in any direction and will not ravel. Stretch nonwovens have crosswise stretch, most effective for knits.

Both woven and nonwoven interfacings are available in *sew-in* and *fusible* versions. Sew-in interfacing must be pinned or basted, and is ultimately held in place by machine stitching. Fusibles have a coating on one side which, when steam-pressed, melts and fuses the interfacing to the wrong side of the fabric. Fusibles come in plastic wrappers which have directions for applying. Follow them precisely, since each fusible is different. When applying fusibles, use a damp press cloth to protect the iron and provide extra steam.

Choosing between fusible and sew-in interfacing is usually a matter of personal preference. Sew-ins require more hand work. Fusibles are quick and easy, and give more rigidity to the garment. However, some delicate fabrics cannot take the heat that fusing requires. Textured fabrics such as seersucker cannot be fused because the texture would be lost.

Interfacings are made in weights from sheer to heavy and usually come in white, gray, beige or black. There are special timesaving interfacings for waistbands, cuffs and plackets. These have pre-marked stitching lines to keep edges even.

Another interfacing aid is *fusible web,* available in strips of various widths. It bonds two layers of fabric together, making it possible to bond a sew-in interfacing to the fashion fabric. Fusible web can also be used to put up hems, hold appliqués in place and secure patches before stitching.

Guide to Interfacings

Fusible woven interfacings are available in different weights and crispness, from medium to heavyweight. Cut them on the same grain as the garment piece, or on the bias for softer shaping.

Fusible nonwoven interfacings come in all weights, from sheer to heavyweight. Stable nonwovens have little give in any direction and can be cut on any grain.

Fusible knit interfacings are made of nylon tricot, which is stable in the lengthwise direction and stretches on the crosswise grain to be compatible with lightweight knit and woven fabrics.

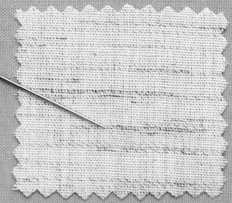

Sew-in woven interfacings preserve the shape and qualities of the fabric, and should be used for natural shaping with woven fabrics. Weights range from sheer organza and batiste to heavyweight hair canvas.

Sew-in nonwovens provide a choice of weight, color, stretch, stable or all-bias combinations. They are appropriate for knits and stretch fabrics as well as for wovens. Preshrink all nonwoven interfacings.

Fusible web is a bonding agent used to join two layers of fabric without stitching. Although it is not an interfacing, it adds some stiffness to the fabric but does not prevent stretching.

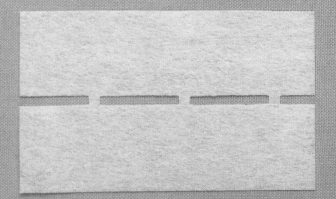

Nonwoven fusible waistbanding is precut in widths or strips to be used for extra firm, crisp edges such as waistbands, cuffs, plackets and straight facings. It has premarked stitching or fold lines.

Nonwoven sew-in waistbanding is a heavyweight, very firm finished strip for stiff, stable waistbands or belts. It is available in several widths. It can be sewn to the back or facing of a waistband, but is too stiff to sew into a waistband seam.

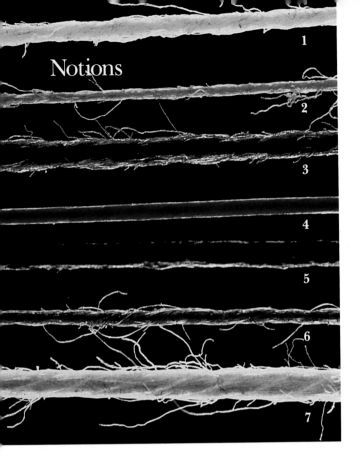

Notions

Thread

Select high-quality thread according to the fiber and weight of the fabric and the purpose of the stitching. As a general guideline, use a natural fiber thread for natural fiber fabrics and synthetic fiber thread for synthetic fabrics. Photo above has been enlarged 20 times to show detail.

1) Cotton-wrapped polyester thread is an all-purpose thread designed for hand and machine sewing on all fabrics: natural fibers and synthetics, wovens and knits.

2) Extra fine cotton-wrapped polyester thread reduces fabric puckering on lightweight fabrics, and does not build up or break during machine embroidery.

3) Topstitching and buttonhole twist is designed for topstitching, decorative programmed stitching, cording in machine-worked buttonholes and stitching hand-worked buttonholes.

4) Hand quilting thread is a strong cotton or polyester/cotton thread that does not tangle, knot or untwist while hand sewing through layers of fabric.

5) Button and carpet thread is suitable for hand sewing where extra strength is required.

6) Long-fiber polyester thread is smooth and even, and suitable for hand or machine stitching.

7) 100% mercerized cotton thread is used for natural fiber woven fabrics like cotton, linen and wool; it does not have enough stretch for knits.

Trims & Tapes

Choose trims and tapes that are compatible with your fabric and thread. Most trims and tapes can be machine stitched, but some must be applied by hand. Preshrink trims for washable garments.

1) Single-fold bias tape, ½" (1.3 cm) wide, and wide bias tape, ⅞" (2.2 cm) wide, available in prints and solid colors, are used for casings, trim and facings.

2) Double-fold bias tape binds a raw edge. It comes in ¼" (6 mm) and ½" (1.3 cm) folded widths.

3) Lace seam binding is a decorative lace hem finish or lace insertion for all fabrics.

4) Seam tape is 100% rayon or polyester, ⅜" (1 cm) wide, used to stay seams, finish hems and reinforce clipped corners.

5) Rickrack comes in ¼" (6 mm), ½" (1.3 cm), and ⅝" (1.5 cm) widths for accent trim and edging.

6) Braid is available in loop (shown), soutache and middy styles. Use it for accent, scroll motifs, drawstrings, ties or button loops.

7) Twill tape is used to stay seams or roll lines.

8) Corded piping is an accent trim inserted in seams to define and decorate edges.

9) Elastic is inserted in casings to shape waistbands, wrists and necklines. Knitted **(9a)** and woven **(9b)** elastics are softer then braided elastics **(9c)**, curl less, and can be stitched directly onto the fabric. Non-roll waistband elastic has lateral ribs to keep it from twisting or rolling.

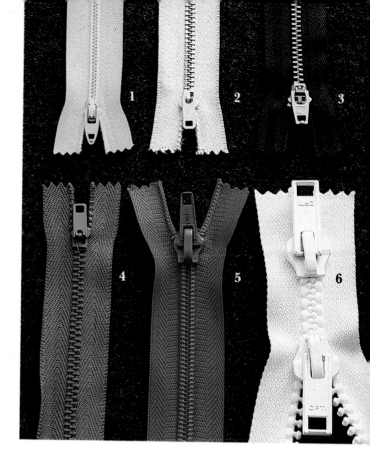

Buttons & Closures

Select these notions either to blend with the garment or stand out and make a fashion statement. Closures can be decorative as well as functional.

1) Sew-through, two-hole or four-hole buttons are commonly-used, all-purpose buttons.

2) Shank buttons have a "neck" or shank underneath the button.

3) Self-covered buttons can be covered with the same fabric as the garment for an exact color match.

4) Toggles are loop-and-bar fasteners with leather or leather-like trim, used on lapped areas.

5) Frogs are loop-and-ball fasteners that lend a dressy look to special outfits.

6) Snap and Velcro® tapes are used as closures on lapped areas of jackets, shirts or casual dresses.

7) Heavy-duty hooks and eyes are used to close waistbands on skirts or pants.

8) Hooks and eyes are inside closures available in sizes appropriate to various fabric weights.

9) Snaps are inside closures for areas that do not receive much stress, such as cuffs.

10) Jumbo snaps are hammered on or applied with a plier-like tool on the outside of a garment for a decorative effect.

Zippers

Zippers have metal or plastic teeth, or a synthetic coil of polyester or nylon attached to a woven tape. Both types come in all-purpose weights. Coil zippers are lightweight, more flexible, heat-resistant and rustproof. Metal zippers come in heavier weights for heavy fabrics and sportswear. Although zippers are usually designed to blend into the garment, some are big, colorful and made to be shown off.

1) Polyester all-purpose zippers are suitable for fabrics of all weights in skirts, pants, dresses and home decorating items.

2) Metal all-purpose zippers are strong, durable zippers for sportswear as well as pants, skirts, dresses and home decorating items.

3) Brass jean zippers are stamped metal zippers with a closed bottom, designed for jeans, work and casual wear in medium to heavyweight fabrics.

4) Metal separating zippers, available in medium and heavy weights, are used in jackets, sportswear and home decorating. Reversible separating zippers have pull tabs on the front and back of the zipper.

5) Plastic molded separating zippers are lightweight yet strong and durable, designed with extra fullness to give a smooth, straight finish to the application. Their decorative appearance makes them a natural for skiwear and outdoor wear.

6) Parka zippers are plastic molded separating zippers with two sliders, so they can be opened from the top and bottom.

Layout, Cutting & Marking

Once you have chosen the pattern and fabric and assembled the proper equipment, you're ready to start creating your garment. Before you cut, make sure the fabric is properly prepared and the pattern correctly laid out.

Much of fabric preparation and layout has to do with the fabric grain. *Grain* is the direction in which the fabric threads run.

Woven fabrics consist of lengthwise threads intersecting crosswise threads. When these threads cross one another at perfect right angles, the fabric is *on-grain*. If the intersection of lengthwise and crosswise threads does not form right angles, the fabric is *off-grain*. It is essential that your fabric be on-grain before cutting. If fabric is cut off-grain, the garment will never hang or fit correctly.

The direction of the lengthwise threads is called the *lengthwise grain*. This grainline runs parallel to the *selvage*, a narrow, tightly-woven border which runs along both lengthwise sides of the fabric. Because lengthwise threads are stronger and more stable than crosswise threads, most garments are cut so the lengthwise grain runs vertically. The crosswise threads form the *crosswise grain*, which runs at right angles to the selvage. In most fabrics, it has a slight amount of give. Fabrics with border prints are often cut on the crosswise grain so the border will run horizontally across the garment.

Any diagonal line intersecting the lengthwise and crosswise grains is called a *bias*. Fabric cut on the bias has more stretch than fabric cut on the grainline. A *true bias* is formed when the diagonal line is at a 45-degree angle to any straight edge. This angle provides the most stretch. Strips cut on the true bias are often used to finish curved edges such as necklines and armholes. Plaids and stripes can be cut on the bias for an interesting effect. Garments cut on the true bias usually drape softly.

Knit fabrics are formed by interlocking loops of yarn called *ribs*. The ribs run parallel to the lengthwise sides of the fabric. Their direction can be compared to the lengthwise grain of woven fabrics. The rows of loops at right angles to the ribs are called *courses* and are comparable to the woven crosswise grain. Knits have no bias and no selvage. Some flat knits have perforated lengthwise edges that look something like a selvage, but these cannot be relied on to establish true lengthwise grain. Knits have the most stretch in the crosswise direction, and are cut with the crosswise grain running horizontally around the body for maximum comfort.

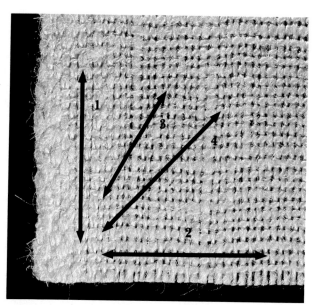

Woven fabrics have lengthwise (**1**) and crosswise (**2**) threads. The lengthwise threads are stronger, since they must withstand greater tension during weaving. Bias (**3**) is any diagonal direction. True bias (**4**) is a 45-degree angle. It has the most stretch.

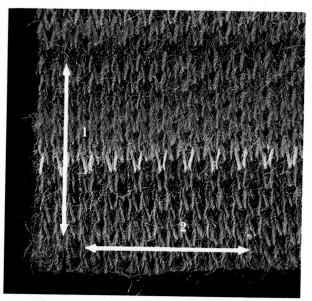

Knit fabrics have lengthwise (**1**) ribs parallel to the length of the fabric. Crosswise courses (**2**) run at right angles to the ribs. Some knits are flat. Others are made in a tubular shape; these can be cut open along a lengthwise rib if a single thickness is needed for layout.

Preparing the Fabric

Before laying out the pattern, take the necessary steps to prepare the fabric for cutting. The label on the bolt tells whether the fabric is washable or dry-cleanable and how much, if any, the fabric will shrink. If the fabric has not been preshrunk by the manufacturer, or if the label says it will shrink more than one per cent, you must preshrink the fabric before cutting. It is often advisable to preshrink knits, since this removes the sizing that sometimes causes skipped stitches. Zippers and trims may also need preshrinking. Dry-cleanable fabrics can be preshrunk by steam pressing or by a professional dry cleaner. This is especially important if you plan to use fusible interfacing, which requires more steam than normal pressing and may cause shrinkage.

To make sure the fabric is on-grain, begin by straightening the crosswise ends of your fabric. This may be done by pulling a crosswise thread, or cutting along a woven design or crosswise rib of a knit. Next, fold the fabric lengthwise, matching selvages and crosswise ends. If the fabric bubbles, it is off-grain. Fabric that is slightly off-grain can be straightened by steam pressing. Pin along selvages and both ends, matching edges. Press from the selvages to the fold. Fabric that is very much off-grain must be straightened by pulling fabric in the opposite direction from the way the ends slant. Permanent-finish fabrics cannot be straightened.

How to Preshrink Fabric

Preshrink washable fabric by laundering and drying it in the same manner you will use for the finished garment. You may also immerse it in hot water. After 30 minutes to one hour, gently squeeze water out and dry fabric as you would the finished garment.

Steam press to preshrink dry-cleanable fabrics. Steam evenly, moving iron horizontally or vertically (not diagonally) across the grain. After steaming, let fabric dry on smooth, flat surface for four to six hours, or until thoroughly dry.

How to Straighten Crosswise Ends of Fabric

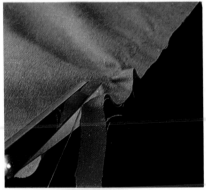

Pull threads to straighten woven fabric. Clip one selvage and gently pull one or two crosswise threads. Push fabric along threads with your other hand until you reach opposite selvage. Cut fabric along pulled thread.

Cut on a line to straighten a stripe, plaid, check or other *woven* design. Simply cut along a prominent crosswise line. Do not use this method for *printed* designs, because they may be printed off-grain.

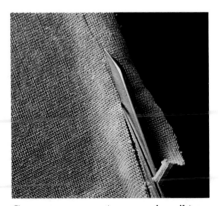

Cut on a course (a crosswise rib) to straighten ends of a knit. It may be easier to follow along the course if you first baste-mark it with contrasting thread, or mark with marking pencil or chalk.

Laying Out the Pattern

Get ready to lay out the pattern by preparing a large work area such as a table topped with a cutting board, or other large flat surface. Assemble all the pattern pieces for the view you are making and press them with a warm, dry iron to remove wrinkles.

Locate the correct layout diagram on the pattern direction sheet. Pattern layouts are reliable guides for laying out the pattern quickly and efficiently. Find the layout for the view, fabric width and pattern size you are using. When working with a napped or other directional fabric (page 49), choose a "with nap" layout. Circle the layout with a colored pen to make sure you refer to the correct layout each time.

Fold the fabric as indicated on the layout. Most fabrics are cut with the right side folded in. This makes it easier to mark and faster to stitch, since some pieces will be in position to sew. Cottons and linens are usually folded right side out on the bolt; wools, wrong side out. The right side of the fabric may appear shinier or flatter, or have a more pronounced weave. Selvages look more finished on the right side. If you cannot tell which is the right side, simply pick the side you like best and consistently use that as the right side. A slight difference in shading that is not apparent as you cut may be noticeable in the finished garment if two different sides are used.

The layout diagram indicates the placement of the selvages and fold. Most garments are cut with the fabric folded along the lengthwise grain. If the fabric is to be cut folded on the crosswise grain, the fold is labeled "crosswise fold" on the layout. The crosswise fold should not be used on napped or other directional fabrics.

Place the pattern pieces on the fabric as indicated in the layout. The symbols and markings used in layout diagrams are standardized for all major pattern companies. A white pattern piece indicates that this piece is to be cut with the printing facing up. A shaded piece should be cut with the printing facing down. A dotted line indicates that a pattern piece should be cut a second time.

When a pattern piece is shown half white and half shaded, it should be cut from folded fabric. Cut the other pieces first and refold the fabric to cut this piece. A pattern piece shown extending beyond the fold is cut from a single layer rather than the usual double layer of fabric. After cutting the other pieces, open the fabric right side up and position this piece by aligning the grainline arrow with the straight grain of the fabric.

After all pattern pieces are in place, pin them to the fabric according to the directions below. Do not begin cutting until all pattern pieces are in place.

How to Pin Pattern Pieces in Place

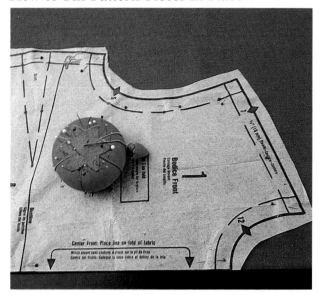

1) Position pattern pieces to be cut on the fold first. Place each directly on folded edge of fabric. Pin corners of pattern diagonally. Continue pinning in the seam allowance, placing pins parallel to the cutting line. Space pins about 3" (7.5 cm) apart, closer together on curves or on slippery fabrics.

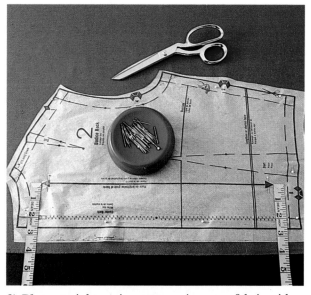

2) Place straight-grain pattern pieces on fabric with grainline arrow parallel to the selvage of woven fabrics, parallel to a rib for knits. Measure from each end of the arrow to the selvage or rib, shifting the pattern until the distances are equal. Pin both ends of the grainline so pattern will not shift. Continue pinning as directed in step 1.

Laying Out
Plaids & Stripes

Select simple styles for plaids and stripes. Complicated fashions can detract from or distort the fabric design. Avoid diagonal bustline darts, long horizontal darts and patterns designated "not suitable for plaids and stripes."

Always buy extra yardage to allow for matching the design at the seams. The extra amount needed depends on the size of the *repeat* (the four-sided area in which the pattern and color of the design are complete) and the number and lengths of major pattern pieces. Usually an extra ¼ to ½ yard (.25 to .50 m) is sufficient.

It is easier to work with even plaids and balanced stripes than uneven plaids and unbalanced stripes. *Even plaids* have the same arrangement of colors and stripes in both lengthwise and crosswise directions. The area of repeat is perfectly square. In *uneven plaids,* the color and stripes form a different arrangement in the lengthwise or crosswise direction, or both. *Balanced stripes* repeat in the same order in both directions; *unbalanced stripes* do not. To match at the seams, all uneven plaids and some unbalanced stripes must be cut from a single layer of fabric, using each pattern piece twice. This doubles the cutting time.

To determine if a plaid is even or uneven, fold back one corner diagonally through the center of a repeat (opposite). In an even plaid, the lengthwise and crosswise color bars will match. An uneven plaid will not match in one or both directions. If the color bars match diagonally, test the plaid one more way to make sure it is even. Fold the fabric vertically or horizontally through the center of a repeat. The halves will form a mirror image if the plaid is even. Some uneven plaids will pass the diagonal test, but fail the vertical/horizontal test.

To make the finished garment look blanced, make sure the dominant color bars, lengthwise and crosswise, are correctly placed. Follow these guidelines:

Position prominent vertical color bars at the center of sleeves, yokes and collars.

Place dominant horizontal bars on or close to garment edges such as hemline and sleeve edges, except in flared styles. Avoid placing dominant horizontal bars across the fullest part of the bust or hips, or at the waistline, because this makes these figure areas look larger.

Match vertical bars of the jacket to vertical bars of the skirt in a two-piece outfit. Place the dominant vertical bar at the center front and back of each piece.

Although it is not always possible to match the design at every seam,

try to match: crosswise bars at vertical seams such as center front and back, and side seams; set-in sleeves to the bodice front at armhole notches; lengthwise stripes where possible; and pockets, flaps and other details to the area of the garment they will cover.

When laying out plaids and stripes, match *stitching* lines, not cutting lines. If fabric tends to shift during cutting, pin or use basting tape to keep fabric in place along matched color bars before pinning pattern in place.

How to Determine if Plaid is Even or Uneven

Even plaid has matching stripes and colors when fabric is folded diagonally through center of any repeat. Halves also form a mirror image when plaid is folded vertically or horizontally.

Uneven plaid creates unmatched stripes and colors in one or both directions when folded diagonally through the center of repeat. Some uneven plaids match when folded diagonally, but do not form a mirror image when folded vertically or horizontally through a repeat.

How to Match Even Plaids

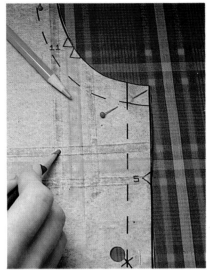  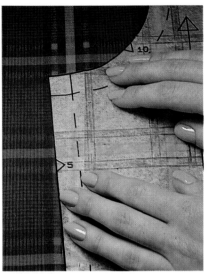

1) Position a front or back pattern piece on the fabric. Trace design of plaid onto pattern piece in the area of a side seam notch. Identify the colors.

2) Place adjoining pattern piece on top of first piece, matching notch and lapping seamlines. Trace plaid design onto reverse side of the second piece.

3) Position second pattern piece on fabric so traced design matches design of fabric. Pin in place. Repeat with other pattern pieces to be matched.

How to Lay Out Plaids

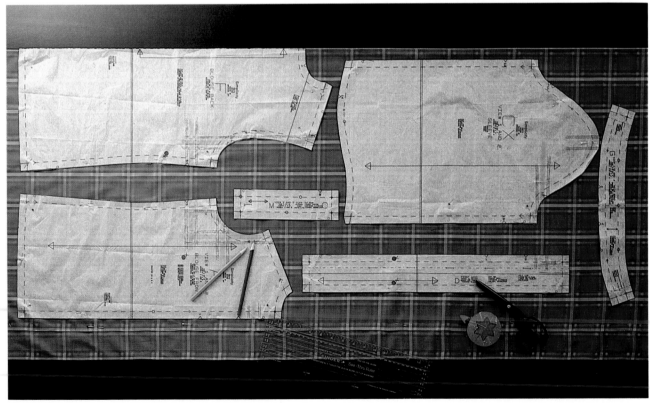

Layout for even plaids can follow either "without nap" or "with nap" diagram on pattern directions, but "with nap" often works best. Notches and symbols along stitching lines should match at sideseams and centers of front and back pieces. Place straight center seams so seamline is directly in the center of the plaid repeat. Place cuffs and pockets so they match the plaid on the portion of the garment they will cover. For two-piece garments, place center fronts and backs of both pieces along the same dominant color bar of the plaid.

Laying Out Directional Fabrics

Directional fabrics include *napped* fabrics such as corduroy, velveteen and flannel; *plush* fabrics such as fake fur; *shiny* fabrics such as taffeta and satin; and *print* fabrics which have one-way designs. Other fabrics which can be directional include some *twill weave* fabrics such as denim and gabardine, and *knits* such as jersey, single or double knits which appear lighter or darker depending on the direction of the grain.

To prevent the garment from having a two-toned look or having its design running in two different directions, all pattern pieces must be laid out with their tops facing the same direction. Napped fabrics can be cut with the nap running either up or down. Nap running up gives a darker, richer look. Nap running down looks lighter and usually wears better. Plush fabrics look best with the nap running down. Shiny fabrics can be cut in whichever direction you prefer. One-way designs should be cut so that the design will be right side up when the garment is completed.

How to Lay Out Directional Fabrics

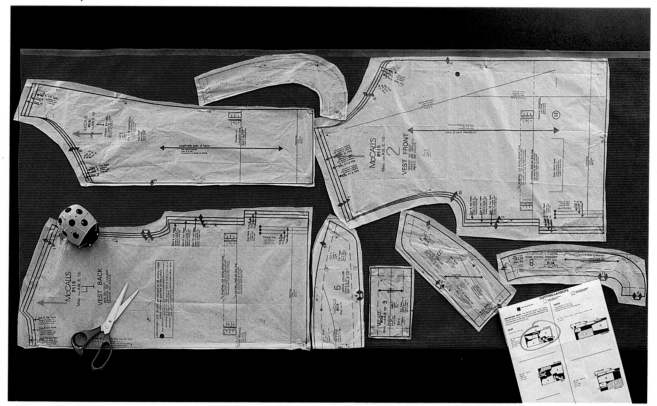

Choose the direction your fabric will run, then lay out the pattern pieces according to the "with nap" layout on the pattern direction sheet. To ensure proper placement, mark each pattern piece with an arrow pointing to the top of the piece. Sometimes the

pattern calls for a crosswise fold. In this case, fold the fabric as the layout indicates, then cut along the foldline. Turn the top layer of fabric around so the nap runs in the same direction as the nap of the lower layer of fabric, and cut both layers at the same time.

Cutting Tips

Arrange your cutting table so you can move around it to get at the pattern from all angles. If your cutting surface is not this accessible, cut groups of pattern pieces apart from the rest of the fabric so you can turn these smaller pieces around.

Accuracy is important, since a mistake in cutting cannot always be corrected. Before cutting, double check placement of pattern pieces and alterations. Before cutting plaids, one-way designs or directional fabrics, make sure the fabric is folded and laid out correctly. Basting tape (page 20) may be helpful to keep fabric from shifting. Heavy or bulky fabric can be cut more accurately one layer at a time. Slippery fabric is easier to cut if you cover the table with a sheet, blanket or other non-slip material.

Choose sharp, plain or serrated blade, bent-handled shears, 7" or 8" (18 or 20.5 cm) in length. Take long, firm strokes, cutting directly on the dark cutting line. Use shorter strokes for curved areas. Keep one hand on the pattern near the cutting line to prevent the pattern from shifting and to provide better control.

The rotary cutter (page 18) is especially useful for cutting leather, slippery fabrics or several layers of fabric. The rotary cutter can be used by either right or left-handed sewers. Use a cutting mat to protect the cutting surface.

Notches can be cut outward from the notch markings, or with *short* snips into the seam allowance (page 53). Be careful not to snip beyond the seamline. Use snips to mark the foldlines and stitching lines of darts and pleats, and the center front and center back lines at the top and bottom. Mark the top of the sleeve cap above the large dot on the pattern with a snip. On bulky or loosely-woven fabric where snips cannot be easily seen, cut pattern notches out into the margin. Cut double or triple notches as one unit, not separately.

After you finish cutting, save scraps to test stitching or pressing techniques, make trial buttonholes or cover buttons. For accurate marking and easy identification, leave each pattern piece pinned in place until you are ready to sew that piece.

Your pattern may call for *bias strips* of fabric to enclose raw edges such as necklines or armholes. Ideally, these are cut from a piece of fabric long enough to fit the area to be enclosed. Bias strips may also be pieced together to form a strip of the correct length.

How to Cut & Join Bias Strips

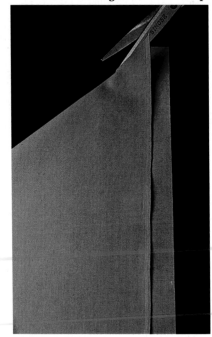

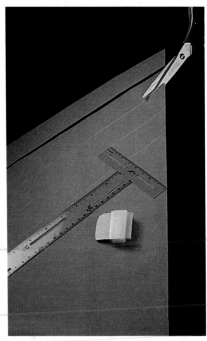

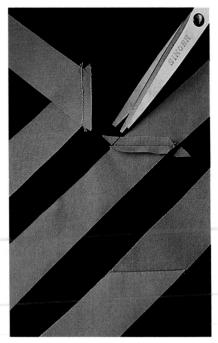

1) Fold fabric diagonally so that a straight edge on the crosswise grain is parallel to the selvage or lengthwise grain. The foldline is the true bias. Cut fabric along the foldline to mark the first bias line.

2) Mark successive bias lines with a marking pencil or chalk, and yardstick or see-through ruler. Cut along marked lines. When a bound finish is called for in a pattern, the pattern will specify the length and width of bias strips needed.

3) Join bias strips if piecing is necessary. With right sides together, pin strips together with shorter edges aligned. Strips will form a "V." Stitch a ¼" (6 mm) seam. Press seam open. Trim points of seams even with edge of bias strip.

Marking Tips

In marking, key pattern symbols are transferred to the wrong side of the fabric after cutting and before the pattern is removed. These markings become continuous reference points to help you through all stages of garment construction. Pattern symbols that should be marked include construction symbols and position marks for placement of details.

Marking is usually done on the *wrong* side of the fabric. Some pattern symbols, such as pocket placement and buttonholes, should be *transferred* from the wrong side to the right side of the fabric (not *marked* on the right side). To do this, hand or machine-baste through the marking on the wrong side. The thread becomes the marking on the right side. Foldlines can be marked by pressing.

There are several ways to transfer markings, each suitable for different fabrics. Choose whichever gives you the fastest, most accurate marking.

Pins are a quick way to transfer markings. They should not be used on fine fabrics or those on which pin marks would be permanent, such as silk or synthetic leathers. Use pin marking only when you plan to sew immediately, since pins may fall out of loose weaves or knits.

Tailor's chalk or dressmaker's pencil, used with pins, are suitable for most fabrics.

Tracing wheel and tracing paper provide a quick, accurate method. It works best on plain, flat-surfaced fabrics. The wheel may damage some fabrics, so always test on a scrap first. Before marking, place a piece of cardboard under the fabric to protect the table. On most fabrics, both layers can be marked at one time.

Liquid markers are felt-tip pens designed especially for fabric. The marker transfers through the pattern tissue onto the fabric. The ink rinses out with water or disappears on its own, so liquid markers can be used on the right side of most fabrics.

Machine basting transfers markings from the wrong side of the fabric to the right side. It can also be used to mark intricate matching points or pivot points. After marking on the wrong side, machine-stitch through the marking. Use a long stitch length or speed-basting stitch, with contrasting color thread in the bobbin. The bobbin thread marks the right side. To mark a pivot point, stitch on the seamline with regular-length stitching and matching thread. Leave the stitching in place as a reinforcement.

Snips or clips can be used on most fabrics except very loosely-woven tweeds and some bulky wools. With the point of a scissors, snip about ⅛" to ¼" (3 to 6 mm) into the seam allowance.

Pressing can be used to mark foldlines, tucks or pleats. It is a suitable method for any fabric that holds a crease.

How to Mark with Chalk, Pencil or Liquid Marker

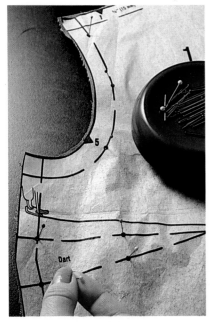

1) Insert pins straight down through pattern and both layers of fabric at marking symbols.

2) Remove pattern carefully by pulling over pin heads. Mark top layer with chalk, pencil or marker at pinpoints on wrong side.

3) Turn fabric over and mark other layer at pinpoints. Remove pins and separate layers.

How to Mark with Basting or Pressing

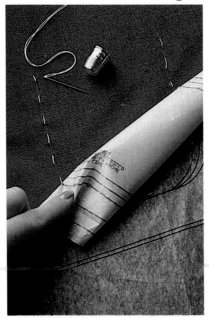

Hand-baste with long and short stitches to mark one layer of fabric. Stitch through pattern and fabric along a solid line, using short stitches on the tissue side and long stitches through fabric. Carefully pull pattern tissue away.

Machine-baste to transfer pencil, chalk or tracing paper markings from the wrong side to the right side. Use contrasting thread in the bobbin, longest stitch on machine. Do not use machine basting on fabrics which mar. Do not press over machine basting.

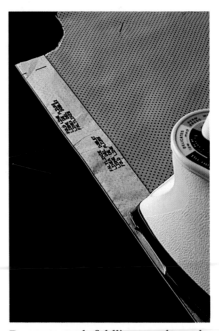

Press to mark foldlines, tucks and pleats. Pin pattern to a single layer of fabric. Fold pattern and fabric along marking line. Press along the fold with a dry iron.

How to Mark with Tracing Wheel & Tracing Paper

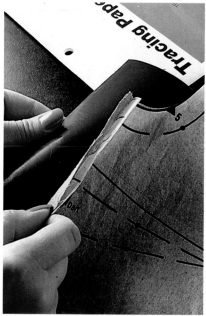

1) Place tracing paper under pattern, with carbon sides facing the wrong side of each fabric layer.

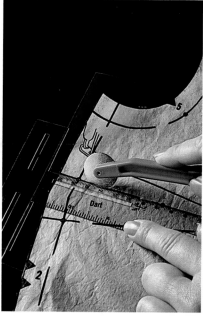

2) Roll tracing wheel over lines to be marked, including center foldlines of darts, using a ruler to help draw straight lines.

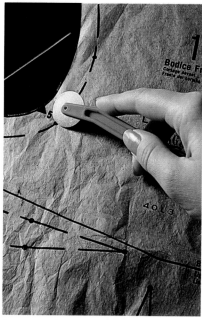

3) Mark dots and other large symbols with short lines perpendicular to the stitching line, or an "X." Use short lines to mark the ends of darts or pleats.

Timesaving Marking Techniques

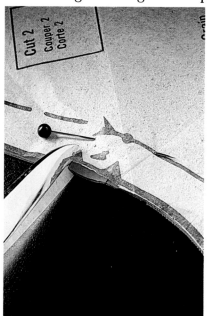

Snips can be used to mark notches, ends of darts, foldlines, or center front and back locations. Make tiny snips, ⅛" (3 mm) deep, into seam allowance. Snip through pattern and both fabric layers with point of scissors.

Pins can mark darts, dots or foldlines without the help of marking pencil. Insert pins through pattern and fabric. Pull pattern carefully over heads. Mark bottom layer with second set of pins. Secure first set of pins to mark top layer.

Tailor tacker has tailor's chalk inserted in two holders. One side has a pin which is inserted through pattern marking to meet chalk on the other side. Twist both sides of tacker so chalk marks two fabric layers in one timesaving step.

Sewing Techniques

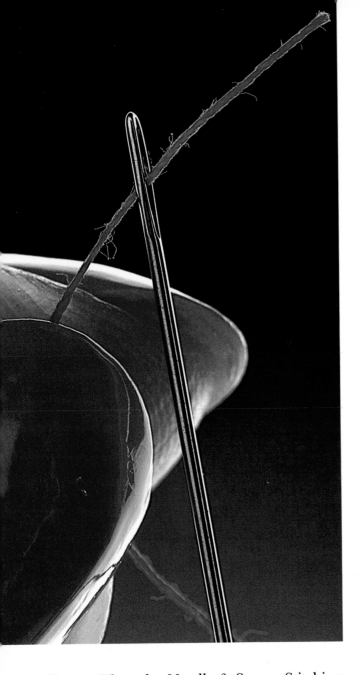

Hand Stitching

Some sewing techniques are best done by hand. These include basting, decorative stitching, tacking and hemming.

For hand stitching, cut an 18" to 24" (46 to 61 cm) length of all-purpose thread. Run it through beeswax to strengthen it and keep it from snarling. Use a short needle (between or quilting) for hemming and a longer needle (milliner's or sharp) for basting.

Running stitch is used for hand basting. It temporarily holds two or more layers of fabric together for fitting or stitching. Beginning sewers may find it easier to hand-baste first, then move on to pin and machine basting.

Backstitch is the strongest of the hand stitches. Use it in hard-to-reach areas, or for understitching where machine stitching would be difficult. It has the appearance of.machine stitching on one side and overlapping stitches on the underside.

Prickstitch is a variation of the backstitch, with tiny stitches on the right side. It is used for decorative topstitching or inserting a zipper by hand.

Slipstitch is an almost invisible stitch, used to hem, tack facings and finish waistbands. It is used with a clean-finished or folded edge.

Catchstitch can be worked flat over a raw edge for tacking. It can also be used as a hemming stitch for lined garments. The *blind catchstitch* is hidden between garment and hem, and is particularly good for knits because it remains flexible.

Blindstitch is worked between the hem and garment, so stitches are not visible. This stitch also helps keep the top of the hem from making a ridge on the right side of the garment.

How to Thread a Needle & Secure Stitching

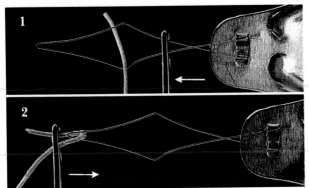

1) Insert wire of a needle threader through eye of the needle. Pass thread through wire loop. **2)** Draw wire through needle eye to pull thread through.

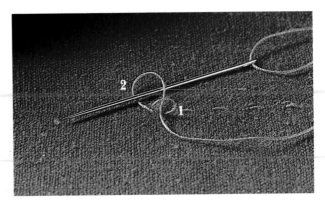

Secure hand stitching with a backstitch at beginning or end of stitching: Take a tiny stitch on wrong side. Pull the thread to form a small loop (**1**). Insert needle through loop, pulling thread to form a second loop (**2**). Insert needle through second loop and pull thread taut.

Straight Stitches

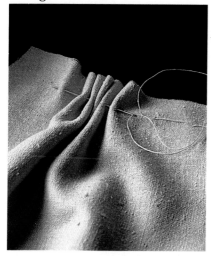

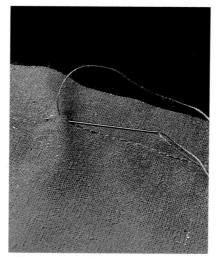

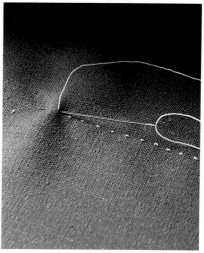

Running stitch. Take several running stitches onto the needle before pulling it through fabric. Secure end of stitching with a backstitch (opposite). Short, even stitches of ¼" (6 mm) give close control. Uneven basting, which combines a long stitch of ½" (1.3 cm) and a short stitch, can be used for straight or slightly curved seams.

Backstitch. Bring needle and thread through fabric to upper side. Insert needle ¹⁄₁₆" to ⅛" (1.5 to 3 mm) *behind* the point where thread came out. Bring needle forward and out the same distance in *front* of that point. Continue inserting and bringing up needle half a stitch length behind and in front of previous stitch. Stitches on underside will be twice as long as those on upper side.

Prickstitch. Bring needle and thread through fabric to upper side. Insert needle through the fabric, one or two fabric threads *behind* point where thread came out. Bring needle up ⅛" to ¼" (3 to 6 mm) in *front* of the point where the thread emerged. The top surface stitches should be very small "pricks".

Hemming Stitches

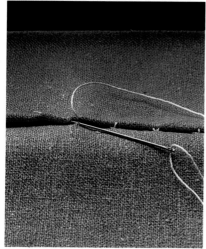

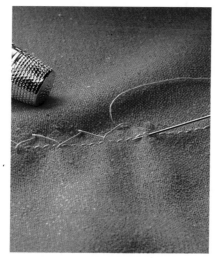

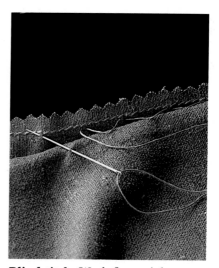

Slipstitch. Work from right to left, holding the folded edge in your left hand. Bring the needle up through the fold. Take a stitch into the garment directly opposite the point where thread came out, catching one or two threads. Slip needle through fold a distance of about ¼" (6 mm). Continue taking stitches about ¼" (6 mm) apart.

Catchstitch. Work from left to right with needle pointing left. Take a small horizontal stitch in hem edge. Take another small horizontal stitch in garment, about ¼" (6 mm) to the right of first stitch, crossing the stitches. Alternate stitches in a zigzag pattern. Work the blind catchstitch like the blindstitch, folding hem away from you.

Blindstitch. Work from right to left with needle pointing left. Roll hem edge back about ¼" (6 mm). Take a very small horizontal stitch in the garment. Take the next stitch in the hem, ¼" to ½" (6 mm to 1.3 cm) to the left of first stitch. Continue alternating stitches. Be careful to keep the stitches in the garment side very small, and do not pull too tightly.

Machine Stitching Tips

Many traditional hand-sewing techniques can now be done completely by machine. Sewing an entire garment by machine is the quickest way to sew. Study your sewing machine manual to become familiar with the available stitches.

As you start to stitch, hold threads behind sewing machine needle so they won't get caught in the feed.

Use the correct throat plate. The straight-stitch plate helps keep sheer fabrics like voile, batiste or lightweight knits from pulling into the feed. Use it only for straight stitching with the straight-stitch foot.

Use a seam guide to help keep seam allowances even. It attaches to the machine bed and adjusts for seams from ⅛" to 1¼" (3 mm to 3.2 cm) wide. The seam guide swivels for sewing curved seams, and is especially useful for very narrow or very wide seams.

Stitch at an even speed appropriate to the fabric and type of stitching. Stitch long seams at full speed, curves and corners slowly.

Do not sew over pins. Never place pins on the underside of the fabric where they could come in contact with the feed.

Use the appropriate attachment for the sewing task. Consult your machine manual if you are unsure of which attachment to use.

Backstitch or tie ends (opposite) to secure stitching at the start and end of the stitching line. This prevents stitches from pulling out.

Use the continuous stitching technique (opposite) to save time when sewing seams and staystitching.

How to Backstitch

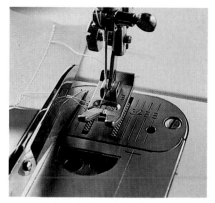

1) Position needle ½" (1.3 cm) from top edge of fabric. Lower presser foot and adjust machine to stitch in reverse. Backstitch almost to edge.

2) Change setting to forward and stitch seam. Stitch just to edge of fabric, not beyond. Set machine to reverse and backstitch approximately ½" (1.3 cm).

3) Raise needle and remove fabric by drawing it to the back and left of needle. Clip threads close to end of stitching.

How to Tie Ends

1) Clip threads, leaving 4" (10 cm) ends. Hold threads in left hand and form a loop. With right hand, bring thread ends through loop.

2) Hold ends in left hand. Insert pin into loop. Work loop down to fabric.

3) Pull thread ends until loop forms a knot. Remove pin. Clip threads close to knot.

How to Do Continuous Stitching

1) Stitch to end of one seam or section. Stitch off edge of fabric. Stitch on to the next section without cutting threads or raising the presser foot.

2) Continue stitching as many seams or sections as possible without stopping.

3) Cut the chain of thread between each section. Press all seams open at once.

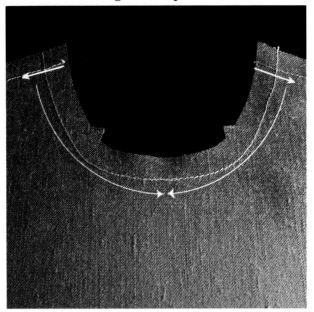

Staystitching is a line of regular machine stitching placed ½" (1.3 cm) from the seam edge on a single layer of fabric. Use it on curves and angles such as necklines, hiplines or waistlines to prevent them from stretching while handling. Stitch with the grain, or *directionally,* usually from widest to narrowest part of the garment.

Bastestitching (1) is the longest stitch on the machine, used to temporarily hold two or more layers of fabric together for stitching, pressing or fitting. Some machines have an extra long speed-basting stitch **(2)**. To make stitches easier to remove, loosen upper tension before machine basting.

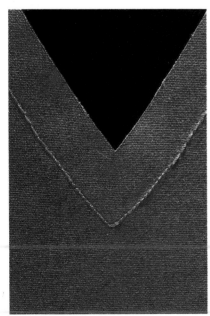

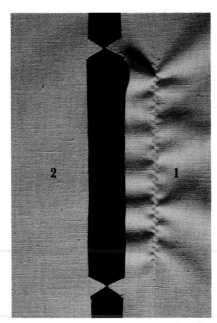

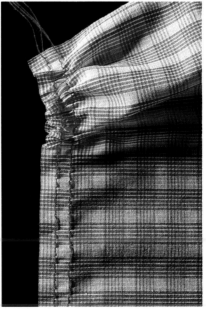

Reinforcement stitching is 18 to 20 stitches per inch (2.5 cm), placed on the seamline to strengthen the fabric at points of strain. It is also used at corners or curves that must be clipped, such as the "V" of a V-neckline or the right angles of a square neckline.

Easestitching is a row of stitching placed on the seamline of a single layer of fabric when slight fullness in one side of a seam **(1)** must be pulled up slightly to evenly fit an edge with no fullness **(2)**. Use long stitches and loosen tension slightly.

Gathering stitch is a line of long stitches placed on the seamline. To add better control, a second row of stitching is usually placed in the seam allowance, ¼" (6 mm) from the first row. Loosen the upper tension slightly before stitching. To gather, pull up the bobbin threads.

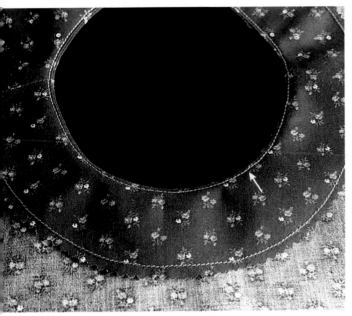

Understitching is straight stitching used to keep facings from rolling to the right side. Trim, clip and press seam allowance toward the facing. Then stitch on the right side of the facing, close to the seamline.

Topstitching is stitching on the right side of the garment. Sew from the right side with all-purpose thread, or topstitching and buttonhole twist thread. Lengthen the stitch slightly, and loosen the tension for a more pronounced stitch.

Two Ways to Rip Stitches

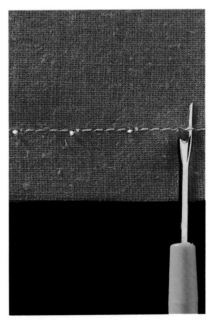

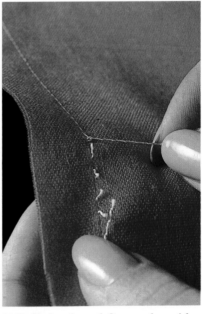

Insert point of seam ripper under stitches. Gently rip one or two stitches at a time, keeping fabric edges taut. *Do not* slide the ripper along the seam. Use this technique when stitching line is hidden.

1) Rip an exposed seam by cutting the stitches on one side of the seam at ½" to 1" (1.3 to 2.5 cm) intervals with a seam ripper or sharp pointed scissors.

2) Pull the thread from other side of seam. Remove threads from the first side with brush or tape.

Seams

A seam is the basic element in all garment construction. It is created by stitching two pieces of fabric together, usually ⅝" (1.5 cm) from the cut edge. Perfect seams are the most obvious sign of a well-made garment. Puckered, crooked or uneven seams spoil the fit as well as the look.

In addition to holding a garment together, seams can be used as a design element. Seams placed in unusual locations or topstitched with contrasting thread add interest to a garment.

Most plain seams require a *seam finish* to prevent raveling. A seam finish is a way of treating or enclosing the raw edges of seam allowances so they are more durable and do not ravel.

Variations of the plain seam include *bound, encased, topstitched* and *eased* seams. Some, such as the flat-fell seam, add strength or shape. Others, such as French or bound seams, improve the appearance of the garment or make it longer wearing.

Techniques for Machine Stitching Seams

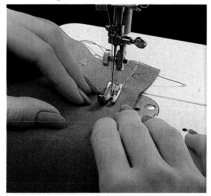

Position the bulk of the fabric to the left of the machine needle, with cut edges to the right. Support and guide fabric gently with both hands as you stitch.

Use guidelines etched on the throat plate of the machine to help you sew straight seams. For extra help, use a seam guide or strip of masking tape placed the desired distance from the needle.

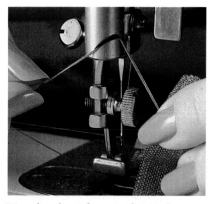

Use the thread cutter located at the back of the presser bar assembly to cut threads after stitching. Or use a thread clipper to cut threads.

How to Sew a Plain Seam

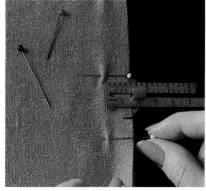

1) Pin seam, right sides of fabric together, at regular intervals, matching notches and other markings precisely. Place pins at right angles to seamline, usually ⅝" (1.5 cm) from edge, with points just beyond seamline and heads toward cut edge for easy removal.

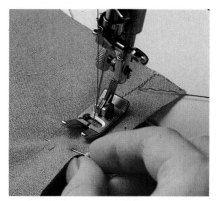

2) Secure stitching with backstitching (page 59). Then stitch forward on seamline, removing pins as you come to them. Backstitch ½" (1.3 cm) at end to secure the stitching. Trim threads.

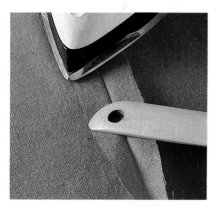

3) Press over stitching line on wrong side to press seam flat. This blends stitches into fabric. Then press seam open. Use your fingers or the blunt end of a point turner to open seams as you press. If seam is curved, such as hip area of skirt or pants, press over curved area of a tailor's ham.

Seam Finishes

A seam finish lends a couture touch and improved appearance to any garment. Finish seams to prevent woven fabrics from raveling and knit seams from curling. Seam finishes also strengthen seams and help them stand up to repeated washings and wearing, making the garment look new longer.

Seams should be finished as they are stitched, before being crossed by another seam. A finish should not add bulk or show an obvious imprint on the right side of the garment after it is pressed. If you are not sure which seam finish to use, try several on a fabric scrap to see which works best.

The seam finishes shown here all begin with a plain seam. They can also be used as edge finishes for facings and hems.

Selvage finish requires no extra stitching. Appropriate for straight seams of woven fabrics, it requires adjusting the pattern layout so that the seam is cut on the selvage.

Stitched and pinked seam finish is suitable for firmly-woven fabrics. It is a quick and easy finish that prevents raveling and curling.

Turned and stitched finish (also called *clean-finished*) is suitable for light to mediumweight woven fabrics.

Zigzag seam finishes prevent raveling and are good for knits, because they have more give than straight-stitched finishes. These finishes use the built-in stitches on automatic zigzag machines.

Basic Seam Finishes

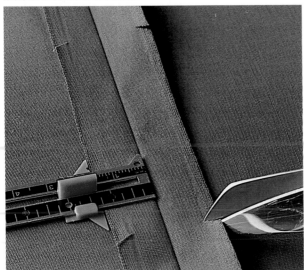

Selvage finish. Adjust pattern layout so that edges of seam are cut on selvage. To prevent shrinking and puckering, clip diagonally into both selvages at 3" to 4" (7.5 to 10 cm) intervals after seam is stitched.

Stitched and pinked finish. Stitch ¼" (6 mm) from edge of each seam allowance. Press seam open. Trim close to stitching with pinking or scalloping shears.

How to Sew a Turned & Stitched Finish

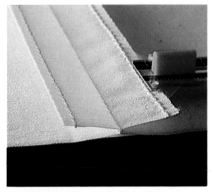

1) Stitch ⅛" to ¼" (3 to 6 mm) from edge of each seam allowance. On straight edges, this stitching may not be necessary.

2) Turn under seam allowance on stitching line. The stitching helps the edge turn under, especially on curves.

3) Stitch close to edge of fold, through seam allowance only. Press seam open.

How to Sew a Zigzag Finish

1) Set zigzag stitch for maximum width. Stitch near, but not over, edge of each seam allowance.

2) Trim close to stitching, being careful not to cut into stitching.

Other Zigzag Finishes

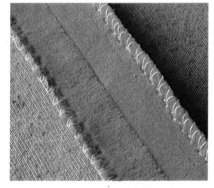

Overedge zigzag finish. Trim seam edges evenly, if necessary. Adjust zigzag stitch length and width to suit fabric. Stitch close to edge of each seam allowance so that stitches go over the edge. If fabric puckers, loosen tension by turning to a lower number.

3-step zigzag finish. Use stitch that puts three short stitches in space of one zigzag width. Set machine for pattern stitch and adjust length and width to suit fabric. Stitch close to edge of seam allowance, being careful not to stretch fabric. On some machines, a *serpentine* stitch gives same results. Trim close to stitching line.

Overedge stretch stitch finish. Trim seam edges evenly. Set machine for pattern stitch and attach overedge foot (page 15). Stitch over trimmed edge of seam allowance. If a narrow stitch width is desired on lightweight fabrics, use general-purpose foot.

Bound Seam Finishes

These finishes totally enclose the cut edge of seam allowances and prevent raveling. They also enhance the appearance of the inside of the garment. Bound seam finishes are a good choice for unlined jackets, especially those made of heavy fabrics or those which ravel easily.

The most commonly used bound finishes are the bias bound, tricot bound and Hong Kong finishes. Mediumweight fabrics such as chino, denim, linen, gabardine and flannel, and heavyweight fabrics such as wools, velvet, velveteen and corduroy can utilize any of the three. Begin each of these finishes by sewing a plain seam. Bound finishes can also be used on hem or facing edges.

Bias bound is the easiest bound finish. Use purchased double-fold bias tape, available in cotton, rayon or polyester, to match the fashion fabric.

Tricot bound is an inconspicuous finish for delicate, sheer fabrics or bulky, napped fabrics. Purchase sheer bias tricot strips or cut ⅝" (1.5 cm) wide strips of nylon net or lightweight tricot. The nylon net must be cut on the bias; the tricot, on the crosswise grain for maximum stretch.

Hong Kong finish is a couture technique used on designer clothing, but because it is so easy and gives such a fine finish to the inside of a garment, it has become a favorite of many home sewers.

Bias Bound

Fold bias tape around cut edge of seam, with wider side of tape underneath. Stitch close to edge of inner fold, catching the wider fold edge underneath.

Tricot Bound

Fold sheer tricot strip in half lengthwise and encase cut edge of seam. Stretch strip slightly as you sew, and it will naturally fold over cut edge. Stitch with straight stitch or medium-width zigzag.

How to Sew a Hong Kong Finish

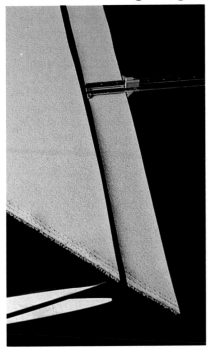

1) Cut bias strips of lining fabric, 1¼" (3.2 cm) wide. Join strips as necessary (page 50) to form strips twice the length of the seams to be finished.

2) Align bias strip on right side of seam allowance. Stitch ¼" (6 mm) from cut edge, stretching bias slightly as you stitch. Use edge of presser foot as stitching guide.

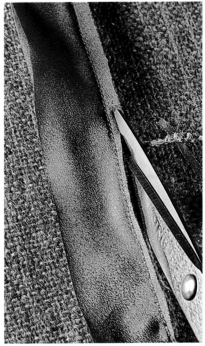

3) Trim seam allowance of heavy fabric to ⅛" (3 mm) to reduce bulk. Lightweight fabric does not need to be trimmed.

4) Press bias strip back over cut edge of seam allowance. Fold bias strip to the underside, enclosing the cut edge.

5) Pin bias strip in place through all layers. Cut edge of bias strip needs no finishing, since a bias cut does not ravel.

6) Stitch in the ditch (the groove where the bias strip and fabric were stitched together). This stitching is hidden on the right side and catches cut edge of bias strip underneath. Press lightly.

Topstitched Seams

Casual, sporty clothes often feature topstitched seams. They provide a decorative touch while holding seam allowances flat. Topstitched seams are also sturdy and durable, because the seam is double or triple stitched.

The most commonly used topstitched seams include: topstitched plain seam, welt, flat-fell, mock flat-fell and lapped. Firm and hard-to-press fabrics such as denim, poplin and knits are suitable for these seams.

Welt seam is often found in suits, coats, sporty dresses and pants. One seam allowance is trimmed and then enclosed by the other seam allowance. This produces a slight ridge and gives a more pronounced look to the seam.

Flat-fell seam is popular in menswear, children's play clothes, denim jeans and reversible and tailored women's garments. It is a sturdy seam which stands up to active wear and repeated washings. Both seam allowances are enclosed so raw edges cannot ravel. The flat-fell seam requires patience and careful attention to detail, because all stitching is done on the right side of the garment. When using this seam, do not mark with snips in the seam allowances.

Mock flat-fell seam, also called the *double-stitched welt seam,* gives the tailored appearance of a flat-fell seam but is much easier to sew. This seam is best for fabrics that do not ravel easily, since one raw edge of the seam allowance is exposed.

Lapped seam can be sewn two ways. One is used to eliminate bulk when stitching interfacing together. The other kind of lapped seam is used on nonwoven fabrics such as synthetic suedes and leathers, or felt.

Topstitch a plain seam by first pressing seam allowances open. From right side, topstitch ¼" (6 mm) from the seamline on each side of the seam. Use the width of the presser foot as a guide. When stitching a wider or narrower distance, use basting tape or quilter bar attachment as a stitching guide.

How to Sew a Welt Seam

1) Stitch a plain seam. Press both seam allowances to one side. Trim the lower seam allowance to just under ¼" (6 mm).

2) Topstitch on the right side, ¼" to ½" (6 mm to 1.3 cm) from the seamline, depending on weight of fabric and desired finished appearance. Stitch through both seam allowances.

3) Finished seam has both seam allowances pressed to one side, but is not bulky because one edge is trimmed and encased.

How to Sew a Flat-fell Seam

1) Pin fabric, *wrong* sides together, at seamline with pin heads toward raw edges. Stitch, taking the usual ⅝" (1.5 cm) seam allowance.

2) Press seam allowances to one side. Trim the lower seam allowance to ⅛" (3 mm).

3) Turn under ¼" (6 mm) on the upper seam allowance and press.

4) Pin folded seam allowance to garment, concealing trimmed lower edge.

5) Edgestitch on fold, removing pins as you come to them.

6) Finished seam is a reversible flat seam with two visible rows of stitching on each side.

How to Sew a Mock Flat-fell Seam

1) Stitch a plain seam. Press seam allowances to one side. Trim lower seam allowance to ¼" (6 mm).

2) Topstitch on right side of garment, ¼" to ½" (6 mm to 1.3 cm) from the seamline. Edgestitch close to the seamline.

3) Finished seam looks like the flat-fell seam on the right side, but has one exposed seam allowance on wrong side.

How to Sew a Lapped Seam in Interfacing

1) Mark seamline with chalk, or snips at both ends of seamline. Lap one edge over the other, matching the seamlines.

2) Stitch on seamline with wide zigzag or straight stitch.

3) Trim both seam allowances close to stitching to eliminate bulk.

How to Sew a Lapped Seam in Nonwoven Fabric

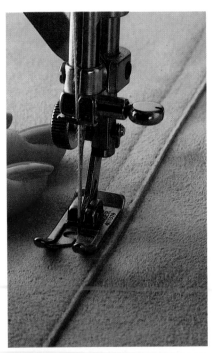

1) Mark seamlines on garment pieces to be joined, with chalk, marking pen or baste-marking. Trim off one seam allowance.

2) Lap trimmed edge over other seam allowance, right sides up, so trimmed edge is exactly on seamline. Tape, pin or glue in place.

3) Edgestitch along cut edge on right side of fabric. Topstitch 1/4" (6 mm) from edge. This gives appearance of flat-fell seam.

Eased Seams

When two garment pieces to be joined are uneven in length, the longer one must be *eased* to fit the shorter one. Eased seams most often occur at shoulder seams, yokes, elbows, waistbands or sleeves. These seams add freedom of movement without adding the bulk of gathers. The mark of perfection in an eased seam is the absence of small tucks or gathers in the seamline. The most common use of an eased seam is a set-in sleeve. It is a basic technique that, with practice, can be performed expertly.

How to Sew an Eased Seam

1) Easestitch on seamline or just slightly inside. Easestitch length is about 8 to 10 stitches per inch (2.5 cm). As you stitch, force the fabric through the machine slightly. This will cause stitching to automatically pull up the fabric.

2) Pin eased edge to shorter edge at each end of seam and at intervals between, matching notches and other markings precisely. Adjust easestitching by pulling up bobbin thread. Pin as often as needed to evenly distribute fullness.

3) Stitch, eased side up, on seamline, removing pins as you come to them.

How to Set in a Sleeve

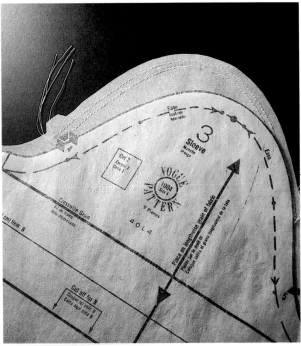

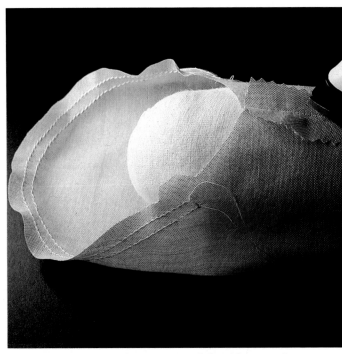

1) Easestitch cap of sleeve (the area between front and back notches) on right side, slightly inside seamline. Easestitch sleeve cap again, ⅜" (1 cm) from edge.

2) Stitch underarm sleeve seam, right sides together. Press seam flat, then press seam open. Use sleeve board or seam roll to prevent impression of seam on top of sleeve.

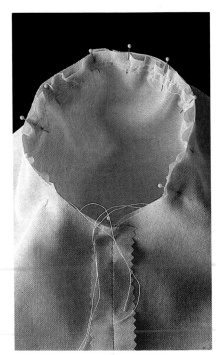

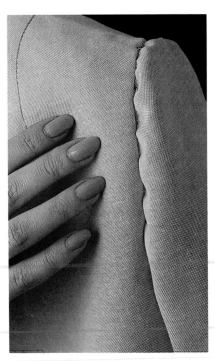

5) Pin sleeve to armhole at close intervals, using more pins in front and back where the bulk of the ease is located.

6) Check sleeve from right side for smooth fit and correct drape. Adjust if necessary. There can be tiny pleats or puckers in seam allowance, but not in seamline.

7) Secure ends of easestitching thread by making a figure-8 over each pin at front and back notches.

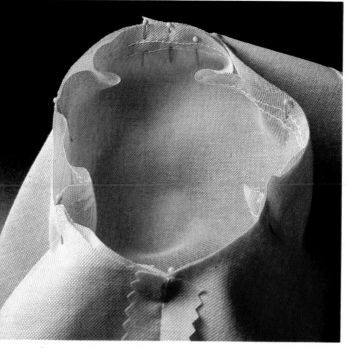

3) Turn sleeve right side out. Turn garment inside out. Insert sleeve into armhole, right sides together, matching notches, small dot markings, underarm seam and shoulder line. Insert pins on seamline for best control of ease.

4) Draw up bobbin threads of easestitching lines until cap fits armhole. Distribute fullness evenly, leaving 1" (2.5 cm) flat (uneased) at shoulder seam at top of sleeve cap.

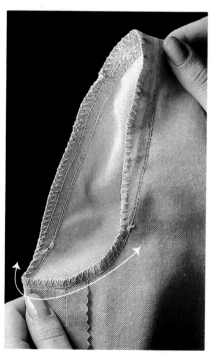

8) Stitch just outside easestitching line, sleeve side up, starting at one notch. Stitch around sleeve, past starting point, to other notch, reinforcing underarm with two rows of stitching. Remove pins as you come to them.

9) Trim seam allowance to ¼" (6 mm) between notches at underarm only. Do not trim seam allowance of sleeve cap. Zigzag seam allowances together.

10) Press seam, allowance of sleeve cap only, using press mitt or end of sleeve board. Do not press into the sleeve.

Curved Seams

Curved seams create a soft fitting line as they shape a flat piece of fabric to the curves of the body. In a *princess seam,* an inward or concave curve is joined to an outward or convex curve. The stitching lines of the two sections to be joined are usually the same lengths; however, the cut edge of the inward curve is shorter and the outward curve is longer than the stitching line. Because these two edges are not the same length, the inward curve must be *clipped* to allow the cut edge to spread before the seam is joined. After the seam is stitched, the outward curve must be *notched* to eliminate excess bulk in the seam when pressed open.

Clipping and notching are used in other curved seams, such as the seam which attaches a straight collar to a curved neckline. Curved collars, cuffs, pockets, flaps or scallops can be quickly clipped and notched at the same time with a pinking shears.

To stitch a curved seam, shorten stitch length and sew slowly for better control. The shorter stitch length also builds extra strength and elasticity into the seam to prevent it from breaking.

Use a seam guide to ensure seams of even width. To accommodate curve, turn seam guide at an angle so the end of the guide is exactly ⅝" (1.5 cm) from the needle.

How to Sew Princess Seams

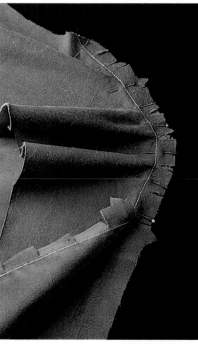

1) Stitch a line of reinforcement stitching (page 60) just inside seamline of inner curve of center panel. Clip into seam allowance all the way to the stitching line at intervals along the curve.

2) Pin inner and outer curves, right sides together with clipped edge on top, spreading clipped inner curve to match all markings and fit outer curve.

3) Stitch on seamline with clipped seam on top, using shorter stitch than usual for the fabric and being careful to keep the lower layer of fabric smooth.

4) Cut out wedge-shaped notches in the seam allowance of outer curve by making small folds in seam allowance and cutting at slight angle. Be careful not to cut into stitching line.

5) Press seam flat to imbed and smooth the stitches. Turn over and press on the other side.

6) Press seam open over curve of tailor's ham, using tip of iron only. Do not press into body of garment. If not pressed to contour, seam lines become distorted and look pulled out of shape.

Stretch Seams

Stretch fabrics for casual or action wear include jersey, stretch terry, stretch velour and other knits. Stretch woven fabrics include stretch denim, stretch poplin and stretch corduroy. For swimwear and leotards, Lycra® knits are available. Seams in these fabrics must stretch or "give" with the fabric. Some sewing machines have special knit stitches that incorporate stretch.

Test the seam or knit stitch on a scrap of fabric to determine its appropriateness to the weight and stretchiness of the fabric. Some of the special knit stitches are more difficult to rip than straight stitching, so be sure the garment fits before stitching. Because knits do not ravel, they usually do not require seam finishing.

Double-stitched seam gives an insurance row of stitching to a seam. Use this method if your machine does not zigzag.

Straight and zigzag seam combines a straight seam with the stretchiness of zigzag. This is a suitable finish for knits that tend to curl along the raw edges.

Narrow zigzag seam is used for knits that do not curl along edges. It is a fast, easy stretch seam.

Straight stretch stitch is formed by a forward/backward motion of reverse-action machines. It makes a strong, stretchy seam appropriate for stressed areas such as armholes.

Straight with overedge stitch has a special pattern which combines a straight stretch stitch with diagonal stitching. It joins and finishes the seam in one step.

Elastic stretch stitch is an excellent choice for swimwear and leotards. The stitch combines a narrow and wide zigzag pattern.

Taped seams are used in areas where you do not want stretch, such as shoulder seams.

How to Sew a Taped Seam

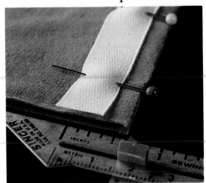

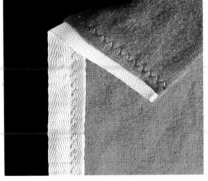

1) Pin fabric, right sides together, so that twill tape or seam binding is pinned over seamline. Position seam binding so it laps ⅜" (1 cm) into the seam allowance.

2) Stitch, using double-stitched, straight and zigzag, overedge or narrow zigzag seam. Press seam open or to one side, depending on selected seam.

3) Trim seam allowance close to stitching, taking care not to cut into seam binding.

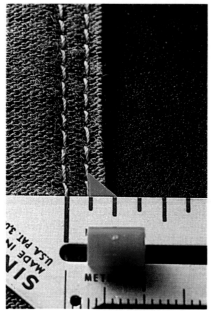

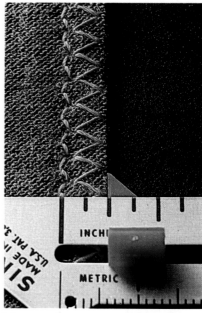

Double-stitched seam. Stitch on seamline with straight stitch, stretching fabric slightly as you sew to incorporate give into the seam. Stitch again, ⅛" (3 mm) into seam allowance. Trim close to second stitching. Press seam to one side.

Straight and zigzag seam. Stitch on seamline with straight stitch, stretching fabric slightly as you sew. Zigzag in seam allowance, close to first row of stitching. Trim seam allowance close to zigzag stitching. Press seam to one side.

Narrow zigzag seam. Set your machine for narrow-width zigzag, 10 to 12 stitches per inch (2.5 cm). Stitch on seamline, stretching fabric slightly. Trim seam allowances to ¼" (6 mm). Press open or zigzag edges together.

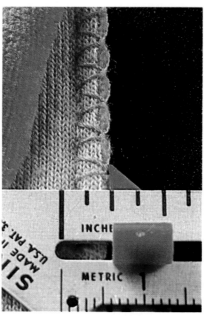

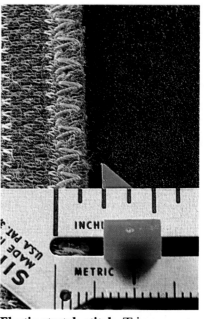

Straight stretch stitch. Stitch seamline with built-in stretch stitch. Guide fabric lightly, letting machine make forward/backward motion. When stitching across folds and seam joinings, assist feeding by holding fabric taut in front and back of presser foot. Trim and press to one side.

Straight with overedge stitch. Trim seam allowances to ¼" (6 mm). Use special overedge foot (page 15) if your machine has one. Place trimmed seam under foot so straight stitches fall on seamline and zigzag stitches fall over seam edge. Press seam to one side.

Elastic stretch stitch. Trim seam to ¼" (6 mm). Place trimmed seam under foot so narrow zigzag falls on seamline and wide zigzag overcasts the seam edge. Press seam to one side.

Building in Shape

Shaping a flat piece of fabric to the curves of your figure can be accomplished with several different shapebuilding techniques. Darts, gathers, pleats and tucks all work to control fabric fullness, but each creates a different effect.

Darts draw the fabric close to the body. Darts at the bust, hips, shoulder line or elbows allow fabric to fit body contours. The point of the dart should always point to the fullest part of the body.

Gathers give a soft, rounded shape. They are easy to fit and comfortable to wear. They may be found at the waistline, sleeves, cuffs, yoke or neckline. Ruffles are gathered fabric strips applied in a seam or at a hem edge. The technique for sewing ruffles is the same as the technique for gathers.

Pleats and tucks are used at waistlines, on the bodice, on shirts, or on sleeves. Both can also be used to control fullness at the sleeve cap or cuff. Stitched pleats offer the same close fit as darts; unpressed pleats give the ease of gathers. In either style, the pleats create a straight, vertical line. Tucks are used either as decoration or as a shaping technique, and can be horizontal, vertical or diagonal.

All these techniques are related because they build in shape. Therefore, they are interchangeable in some cases. For example, darts in a shoulder seam can be replaced with gathers to change a close fit to an eased fit. Unpressed pleats can be replaced by gathers. Released tucks first control fullness, then release it like gathers. You may wish to experiment with substituting one technique for another.

Darts are usually sewn on the inside of the garment. They can be straight or curved. Stitch darts evenly, bring them to a perfect point and press before joining with another garment piece.

Gathers are formed when a larger piece of fabric is drawn up to fit a smaller piece. The hand of the fabric determines whether the gathers look soft or crisp.

Pleats are usually formed on the inside, tucks on the outside of a garment. Accurate marking and stitching are important to ensure that the pleats and tucks are of even width.

Darts

A dart is used to shape a flat piece of fabric to fit bust, waist, hip or elbow curves. There are two types of darts. A *single-pointed dart* is wide at one end and pointed at the other. A *shaped dart* has points at both ends. It is usually used at the waistline, with the points extending to the bust and hips. Besides providing a closer fit, darts are also used to create special designer touches and unique styles.

Perfect darts are straight and smooth, not puckered at the ends. The darts on the right and left sides of the garment should have the same placement and length.

How to Sew a Dart

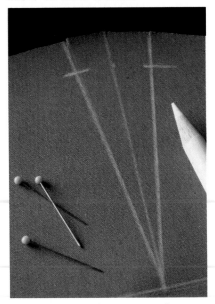

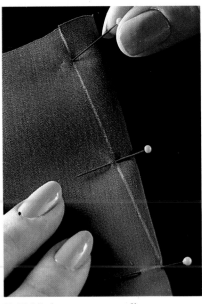

1) Mark dart using appropriate marking method for fabric. Mark point of dart with horizontal line.

2) Fold dart on center line, matching stitching lines and markings at the wide end, the point and in between. Pin in place, with heads of pins toward folded edge for easy removal as you stitch.

3) Stitch from wide end to point of dart. Backstitch at beginning of stitching line, then continue stitching toward point, removing pins as you come to them.

Dart Techniques

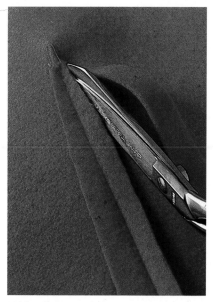

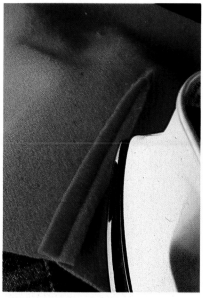

Shaped darts are stitched in two steps, beginning at the waistline and stitching toward each point. Overlap stitching at waist about 1" (2.5 cm). Clip dart fold at waistline and midway along points, to within ⅛" to ¼" (3 to 6 mm) of stitching to relieve strain and allow dart to curve smoothly.

Wide darts and darts in bulky fabrics should be slashed open on the fold line and trimmed to ⅝" (1.5 cm) or less. Slash to within ½" (1.3 cm) of point. Press dart open and press point flat.

Press darts over the curve of a tailor's ham to maintain the built-in curve. Vertical darts are usually pressed toward the center front or center back. Horizontal darts are usually pressed downward.

4) Taper to point of dart. When ½" (1.3 cm) remains, shorten stitch length to 12 to 16 stitches per inch (2.5 cm). Take last two to three stitches directly on fold. Do not backstitch at the point, because this may cause puckering. Continue stitching off edge of fabric.

5) Raise presser foot and pull dart toward front. About 1" (2.5 cm) back from point of dart, lower presser foot and secure thread by stitching several times in fold of the dart with stitch length set at 0. Clip threads close to knot.

6) Press folded edge of dart flat, being careful not to crease fabric beyond the point. Then place dart over curve of tailor's ham and press in proper direction (above). For a neat, flat finish, press darts before they are stitched into a seam.

Gathers

A soft, feminine garment line is often shaped with gathers. They may be found at waistlines, cuffs, yokes, necklines or sleeve caps. Soft and sheer fabrics produce a draped look when gathered; crisp fabrics create a billowy effect.

Gathers start with two stitching lines on a long piece of fabric. The stitching lines are then pulled at each end to draw up the fabric. Finally, the gathered piece is sewn to a shorter length of fabric.

The stitch length for gathering is longer than for ordinary sewing. Use a stitch length of 6 to 8 stitches per inch (2.5 cm) for mediumweight fabrics. For soft or sheer fabrics, use 8 to 10 stitches per inch. Experiment with the fabric to see which stitch length gathers best. A longer stitch makes it easier to draw up the fabric, but a shorter stitch gives more control when adjusting gathers.

Before you stitch, loosen the upper thread tension. The bobbin stitching is pulled to draw up the gathers, and a looser tension makes this easier.

If the fabric is heavy or stiff, use heavy-duty thread in the bobbin. A contrasting color in the bobbin also helps distinguish it from the upper thread.

How to Sew Basic Gathers

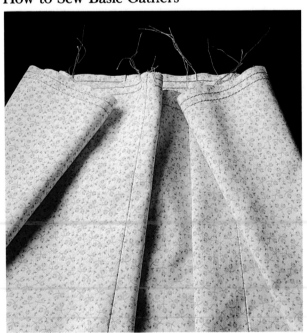

1) Stitch a scant ⅝" (1.5 cm) from raw edge on right side of fabric, starting and ending at seamline. Loosen upper tension and lengthen stitches appropriate to fabric. Stitch a second row in seam allowance, ¼" (6 mm) away from first row. This double row of stitching gives better control in gathering than a single row.

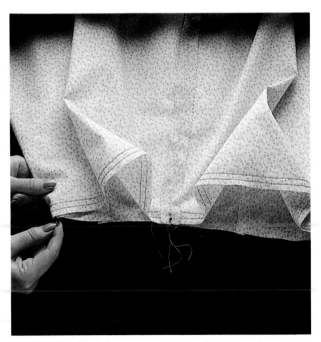

2) Pin stitched edge to corresponding garment section, right sides together. Match seams, notches, center lines and other markings. Fabric will droop between the pinned areas. If there are no markings to guide you, fold straight edge and gathered edge into quarters. Mark fold lines with pins. Pin edges together, matching marking pins.

3) Pull both bobbin threads from one end, sliding fabric along thread to gather. When half the gathered section fits the straight edge, secure bobbin threads by twisting in a figure-8 around pin. Pull bobbin threads from other end to gather remaining half.

4) Pin gathers in place at frequent intervals. Distribute gathers evenly between pins. Reset stitch length and tension for regular sewing.

5) Stitch, gathered side up, just outside gathering lines. Adjust gathers between pins as you stitch. Hold gathers taut with fingers on both sides of needle. Keep gathers even, so folds of fabric do not form as you stitch.

6) Trim seam allowances of any seams that have been sewn into the stitching line, trimming off corners at a diagonal.

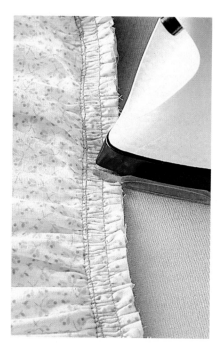

7) Press seam allowance on wrong side, using tip of iron. Then open out garment and press seam in the direction it will lie in the finished garment. Press seam toward gathers for puffy look, toward garment for smoother look.

8) Press into gathers with point of iron on right side of garment, lifting iron as you reach seam. Do not press across gathers; this will flatten them.

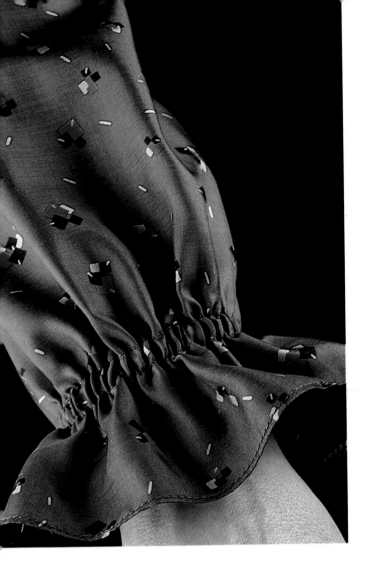

Gathering with Elastic

Gathers formed with elastic offer comfortable and easy fit in knits and active sportswear. This technique ensures uniform gathers and creates shape that is relaxed and not as close to the body as other shapebuilders.

Elastic can be stitched directly to the garment or inserted in a casing. A casing is a tunnel for elastic, created with a turned-under edge or with bias tape stitched to the fabric. Choose an elastic that is suitable to the sewing technique and area of the garment where it is used (page 40).

Elastic in a casing can be any width. Use a firm, braided or non-roll elastic. Braided elastic has lengthwise ribs, and narrows when stretched.

Stitched elastic calls for woven or knitted elastics which are soft, strong and comfortable to wear next to the skin. On short areas such as sleeve or leg edges, it is easiest to apply the elastic while the garment section is flat, before side seams are stitched. When using stitched elastic at a waistline, overlap the ends of the elastic and stitch to form a circle before pinning to the garment.

Cut elastic the length recommended by the pattern. This length includes a seam allowance. To add elastic when the pattern does not call for it, cut the elastic slightly shorter than the body measurement plus seam allowance. Allow 1" (2.5 cm) extra for a stitched elastic seam, ½" (1.3 cm) extra for overlapping elastic in a casing.

How to Sew Elastic in Casing (waistline seam)

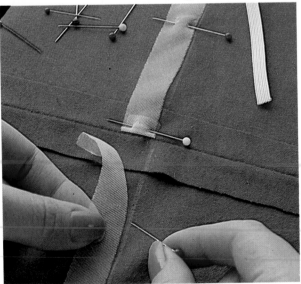

1) Pin sheer bias tricot strip or bias tape that is ¼" (6 mm) wider than the elastic to inside of garment along marked casing lines, beginning and ending at one side seam. Turn under ¼" (6 mm) at each end of bias tape and pin to seamline. For easy application, work on ironing board with garment wrong side out.

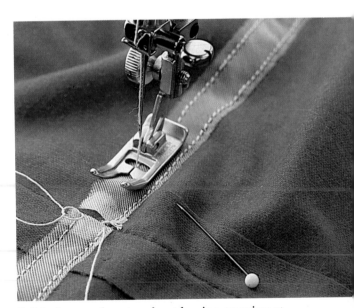

2) Stitch tape close to edges, leaving opening at seam to insert elastic. Do not backstitch at ends of stitching, because this stitching shows on the right side of the garment. Instead, pull all four ends to inside and knot.

How to Sew Stitched Elastic

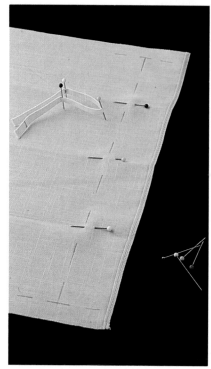

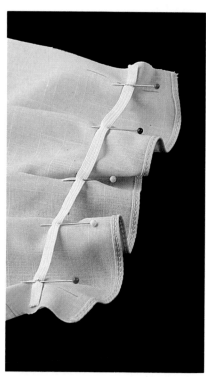

1) Fold elastic and fabric into fourths. Mark fold lines of elastic and garment with pins.

2) Pin elastic to wrong side of garment, matching marking pins. Leave ½" (1.3 cm) seam allowance at each end of elastic.

3) Stitch elastic to fabric, elastic side up, stretching elastic between pins, with one hand behind needle and other hand at next pin. Apply with a zigzag, multi-stitch zigzag or two rows of straight stitching, one along each edge of elastic.

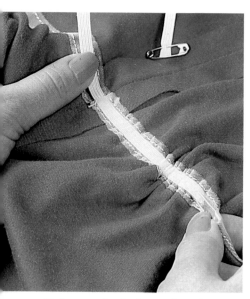

3) Insert elastic through casing using a bodkin or safety pin, taking care not to twist elastic. Place a large safety pin across free end of elastic to prevent it from pulling through.

4) Lap ends of elastic ½" (1.3 cm) and sew together with straight or zigzag stitches, stitching forward, backstitching, and forward again. Clip thread ends. Ease elastic back into casing.

5) Slipstitch ends of casing together. Distribute gathers evenly along the elastic.

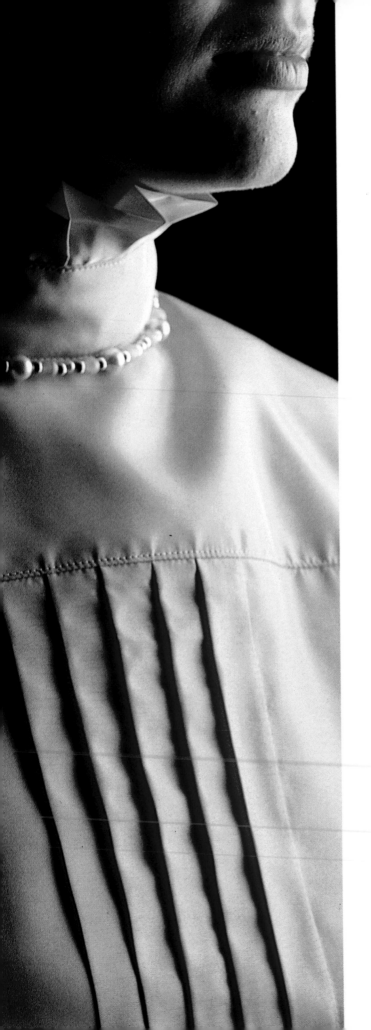

Pleats & Tucks

Like gathers, pleats and some tucks add fullness to a garment. This kind of fullness is controlled and tailored, creating a more sophisticated look than the softness of gathers.

Pleats are folds of fabric which provide controlled fullness. They are always vertical. There are four basic types: *box pleats,* which have two folds turned away from each other; *knife or side pleats,* in which all the pleats are turned to one side; *inverted pleats,* which have folds turned toward each other and meeting; and *accordion pleats,* which have narrow folds resembling the bellows of an accordion, always pressed along their entire length. Accordion pleats are best done by a professional pleater. Other pleats may be pressed or stitched to knife-sharp folds or left unpressed to fall gently.

Accurate marking, stitching and pressing are essential for successful pleats. Use tailor's chalk, marking pencil or thread marking, using different colors to mark foldlines and placement lines. The *foldline* indicates the sharply-creased fold on pressed pleats. The *placement line* is where the folded edge of each pleat is placed and stitched. The *roll line* is used in unpressed pleats and indicates that the pleats will form soft rolls rather than sharp creases.

Tucks are slender folds of fabric stitched along all or part of their length. Those stitched only partway along their length are *released tucks.* Tucks may be horizontal or vertical. They are usually folded on the straight or crosswise grain, with the fold formed on the outside of the fabric. When tucks are used to control fullness rather than add decoration, the fold is on the inside of the garment.

There are three basic types of tucks: *spaced tucks,* which have a space between each tuck; *pin tucks,* which are very narrow tucks; and *blind tucks,* in which each tuck touches or overlaps the next.

Select light to mediumweight fabrics for tucks and pleats. Heavyweight fabrics are usually too bulky. Fabrics like linen, gabardine, poplin, flannel, broadcloth, crepe de chine and lightweight wools are good choices. Choose soft fabrics for unpressed pleats and crisp fabrics that hold a crease well for pressed pleats. Soft fabrics can be made to hold a crease if edgestitched or pressed with spray starch.

The design of the fabric must be considered in sewing tucks and pleats. Solids are always suitable. Stripes and prints can be used if the tucks or pleats do not distort the fabric design. Plaids can be made into interesting pleats, but choose carefully. Before you buy or cut the fabric, form it into pleats by hand to get an idea of what they will look like.

To help stitch tucks and pleats of even width, use a seam guide (page 15), or place masking tape along the stitching line.

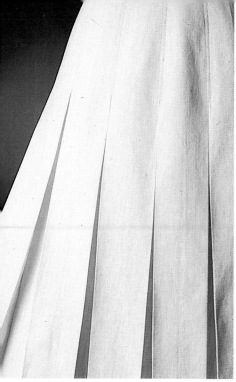

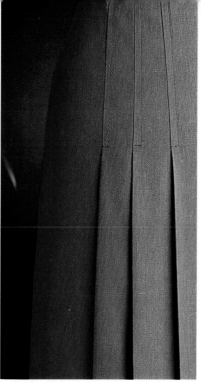

Box pleats may be pressed or unpressed. Unpressed box pleats fall gently into a fuller shape than pressed pleats. Fluid fabrics like cotton, knits, wool, challis and crepe de chine are most suitable for unpressed pleats.

Knife pleats are a tailored and sophisticated touch. Some garments have one cluster of knife pleats facing one way, and another facing the opposite way. Good fabric choices include linen, gabardine and tightly-woven wools.

Inverted pleats create a sporty yet tailored look. The best fabric choices are the same as those for knife pleats.

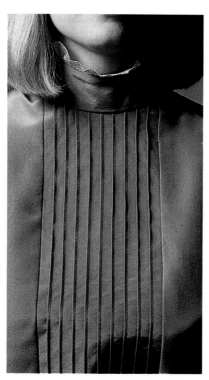

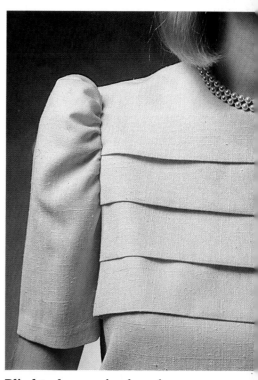

Spaced tucks are an intriguing design feature that can be found across the bodice, near a skirt hem or on sleeves. Most light to mediumweight fabrics work well.

Pin tucks are found on tuxedo-style shirts, tailored dresses and children's wear. The tucks are usually ⅛" (3 mm) wide. Crisp, lightweight fabrics like cotton broadcloth work well.

Blind tucks are a lovely and sophisticated addition to blouses and dresses. The tucks can be almost any width. Most light to mediumweight fabrics are suitable.

How Sew Box & Knife Pleats

1) Mark pleats on wrong side with snips in seam allowance and marking method appropriate to fabric. Form pleats by bringing marked pleat lines together. Pin from hem edge to waist, with fold of pleat to the right (top edge facing you) and pins inserted at right angles to stitching line.

2) Machine-baste each pleat along marked stitching line, from hem to end of pleat (usually indicated by solid lines on pattern piece). At end of pleat, change to regular stitch length and backstitch. Continue stitching to the waistline.

3) Press pleats in the direction they will face. Work on the inside, pressing gently with light steam. Knife or side pleats have all of the backfolds turned in the same direction. The folds of box pleats face each other.

7) Topstitch (knife pleats).
Pin-mark end of pleat on right side of garment. Begin stitching at bottom of pleat. Insert needle ¼" (6 mm) from pleat stitching line. Do not backstitch. Stitch parallel to seamline from pin to top of pleat. Knot threads on inside. To edgestitch and topstitch the same pleat, hem and edgestitch first (steps 10 and 11).

8) Topstitch (inverted or box pleats). Pin-mark end of stitching line. Insert needle exactly at seam. Stitch ⅛" to ¼" (3 to 6 mm) from seam into pleat area. With needle in fabric, raise presser foot and pivot fabric. Lower presser foot and stitch to waist. Stitch both sides in the same direction, from hip to waist. Knot threads on inside.

9) Remove machine basting. Clip threads at backstitching and every 4 to 5 stitches along basting line. Do not remove basting until topstitching is completed, because the basting helps keep the pleats in position for pressing and other construction.

4) Machine-baste pleats in position along upper edge of skirt or pleat section. Stitch on seamline, making sure that all folds are in correct direction. If desired, sew to grosgrain ribbon so stitching does not break during fitting.

5) Place strips of brown paper (cut from heavy grocery bag) under fold of each pleat to prevent an imprint of the pleat on right side of garment. Press to set pleats. Use table-top ironing board or place a table or chair near ironing board to support overhanging fabric.

6) Turn garment to right side. Press pleats in place using press cloth. Unpressed or soft pleats need light pressing, if any. For sharp pleats, use lots of steam and dampened press cloth. Let pleats dry on ironing board.

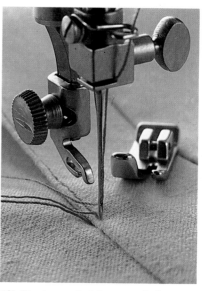

10) Trim seam allowances by half from the cut edge to the hemline, to eliminate bulk before hemming. Finish with appropriate hem. Pleats must be hemmed *before* they are edgestitched.

11) Edgestitch pressed folds of pleats, if desired, for a permanent crisp line. This makes it easier to re-press pleats in washable garments. Stitch from hem to waist, as close to the fold as possible. Inner and outer folds can both be edgestitched.

12) Start topstitching precisely at the point where edgestitching ends, for pleats which are both edgestitched and topstitched. (Presser foot in photo has been removed to show starting point.) Stitch through all thicknesses. Pull all threads to inside and knot.

Three Ways to Mark Tucks

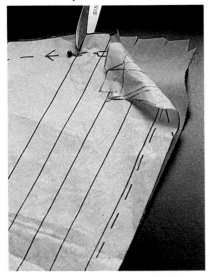

Snip and press to mark tucks on fabrics which hold a crease. Snip into seam allowances about ¼" (6 mm) at both ends of each tuck. Fold between snips and press to mark tucks. Pattern indicates the tuck width.

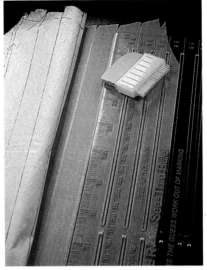

Snip and mark on right side of fabric with water-soluble marking pen, tailor's chalk or chalk marking pencil. Test marking on scrap of fabric to make sure it is removable. Use a ruler or yardstick to connect the snips. Tuck foldline can be marked with one color, stitching line with another.

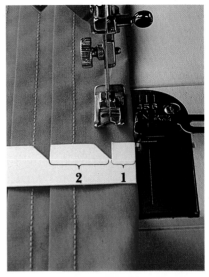

Make a cardboard tucking gauge. Mark foldline of first tuck only, and stitch as directed. On a piece of cardboard, cut a notch as far away from edge as width of tuck **(1)**. Measure width between tuck folds (see pattern) and mark with another notch **(2)**. Place the left-hand notch along fold of stitched tuck. Right edge of gauge marks the next fold; right-hand notch marks the next stitching line.

How to Sew Tucks

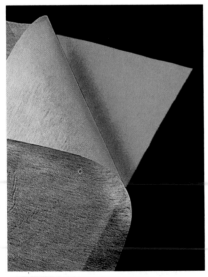

1) Interface area to be tucked with sheerest fusible interfacing. This adds stability and crispness to tucks on slippery, lightweight fabrics such as crepe de chine. These fabrics are difficult to press and stitch evenly. Use straight-stitch foot and needle plate for more accuracy.

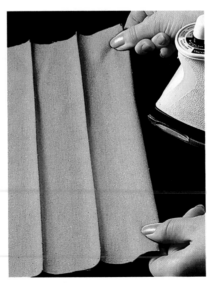

2) Press tucks before stitching if marks have been made with chalk or pencil. Do not press if water-soluble marking pen has been used, because the heat of the iron will set the markings.

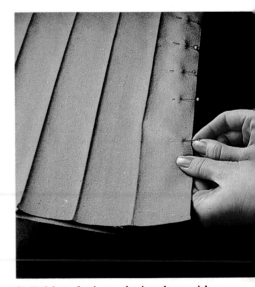

3) Fold and pin tucks in place with pins perpendicular to fold, keeping fold toward right-hand side so pins can be easily removed as you stitch. For slippery fabrics, hand-baste tucks in place.

Tips for Sewing Tucks

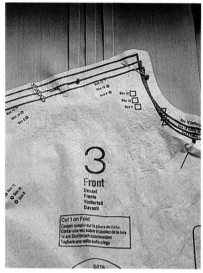

Tucks can be added to a plain garment by stitching tucks in fabric *before* cutting pattern piece. To figure amount of extra fabric needed, multiply width of tuck times two, then multiply by number of tucks to be added. Purchased pre-tucked fabric can also be used to add tucks to a garment area.

Stripes or woven vertical designs are easy to follow for straight stitching. Fold along one part of the stripe and stitch on next stripe. Tucks are usually made on the straight grain.

Twin-needle stitching produces two closely-spaced parallel lines of stitching with narrow pin tuck between. Two different colors of thread can be used for decorative tucks. Tighter tension creates tighter tucks. Some decorative stitches can also be made with the twin needle.

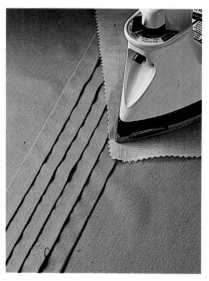

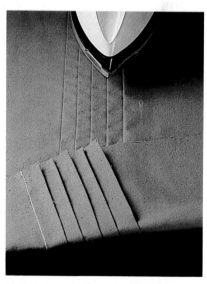

4) Stitch tucks so that upper thread stitching, not bobbin thread, will be visible. Stitch all tucks in the same direction, using presser foot or guidelines on needle plate as a guide. Do not backstitch released tucks. Pull threads to inside and tie.

5) Press the fold of each tuck individually to imbed the stitching. Then press all tucks in one direction. Use a press cloth to avoid marring the fabric.

6) Press tucks in one direction from the wrong side. Use very little steam, and press lightly to prevent the tucks from making indentations in the fabric.

Outer Edges

Outer edges of a garment include hems on lower edges, waistbands, front or back openings, necklines, armholes, collars and cuffs. When finishing outer edges, work to eliminate bulk and achieve a flat, smooth finish. A variety of stitching, trimming and pressing techniques help accomplish this. In most cases, interfacing is used for a crisp, stabilized finish.

An interfaced outer edge requires *facings* — pieces of fabric sewn to the outer edge and turned to the inside to finish the edge. If the edge is shaped or curved, a separate facing is cut and shaped to fit. On straight edges, the facing is often an extension of the pattern piece folded to the inside. Facing edges of unlined garments should be finished to prevent raveling.

Fusible interfacings save time and are available in

weights appropriate for most fabrics. Fusibles are often applied to facings rather than to the garment, because they may create an undesirable ridge on the right side of the garment. Test fusible interfacing on a fabric scrap first. If a ridge forms along the edge of the fused interfacing, trim the outer edge of the interfacing with pinking shears and try again. If a ridge is still noticeable, fuse the interfacing to the facing only. For a more fluid line, choose sew-in interfacings. These are usually applied directly to the garment, not the facing.

In this section, certain techniques include directions for fusible or sew-in interfacings. Specific methods for handling the interfacing can be applied to any of the faced edges and collars that are shown. Cuffs are finished and attached in the same manner as collars.

Faced Necklines & Collars

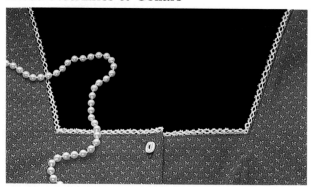

Square necklines must be clipped diagonally into the corners, right up to the line of stitching, so the neckline lies flat when facing is turned to the inside. Neckline edges are understitched or topstitched (page 61) to keep them lying flat.

Round necklines incorporate the techniques used in curved seams. Seam allowances must be *clipped* (snips in the seam allowance up to but not through the stitching line) so the neckline edge lies smoothly when the facing is turned to the inside.

Pointed collars require careful and close trimming of the points to eliminate bulk when collar is turned to the right side. Corners of waistbands, square pockets, tabs and cuffs are other areas requiring close trimming.

Curved collars require *notching* (small wedge shapes cut out of the seam allowance) to reduce bulk. When stitching a curved seam, shorten the stitch length for reinforcement and better control.

How to Face an Outer Edge (using fusible interfacing)

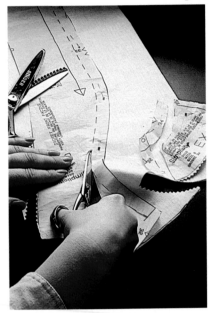

1) Cut out fusible interfacing after cutting facings. Remove seam allowances by cutting on the seamline instead of the cutting line. Trim unnotched edge with pinking shears.

2) Position cut edge of interfacing on seamline on wrong side of garment, adhesive side down. Lightly tack interfacing to garment with point of steam iron at several points around edges.

3) Fuse interfacing in place according to manufacturer's instructions on the interfacing wrapper. For proper bonding, use full amount of time and specified heat setting. Fuse in small sections, overlapping areas where iron is held in place. Do not slide iron.

7) Grade seam allowances by trimming them to graduated widths: facing seam allowance to ⅛" (3 mm), garment seam allowance to ¼" (6 mm). Seam allowance toward garment is wider than the one next to facing, eliminating a bulky ridge.

8) Clip into curve of neckline seam allowances at frequent intervals. Clip up to the stitching line, but not through it. After clipping, hold seam at each end. It should form a straight line; seam allowances should not curl.

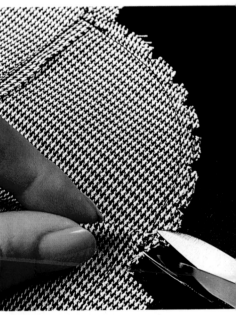

9) Notch seam allowances of outer curved edges by cutting out V-shaped wedges. Be careful not to cut garment. Turn garment to right side. If ripples form in seam allowance, cut additional wedges.

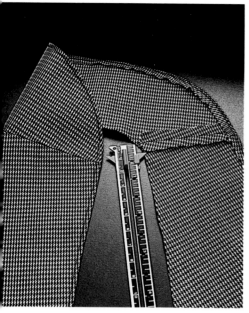

4) Join back and front garment sections and facing sections at shoulder seams. Trim seam allowances of facing to ¼" (6 mm). Press seams open. Do not finish facing seams. Finish garment seams and facing edges with appropriate finish (pages 64 to 67).

5) Stitch right side of facing to right side of garment, matching notches and seams. Stitch in direction of arrows, from center back to lower edge of front facings on each side. Directional stitching maintains the grainline and prevents distortion of curves.

6) Trim corners of seam allowances diagonally where they cross at the shoulder line to eliminate bulk.

10) Turn all seam allowances toward facing and press with point of iron. Be careful to press seam allowances only, and avoid pressing small tucks in garment.

11) Understitch on right side of facing, close to the seamline, stitching through facing and both seam allowances. Keep facing flat, spreading clipped seam allowances of curves so facing will lie flat against garment when turned to inside.

12) Tack facing to shoulder seam with 3 or 4 short stitches between facing and seam allowance. Be careful not to stitch through to right side of garment.

How to Sew a Square Neckline (using fusible interfacing)

1) Remove seam allowances from fusible interfacing, following instructions for faced outer edge (page 96). Fuse interfacing to wrong side of facing, following manufacturer's directions.

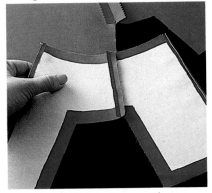

2) Join facing sections and garment sections at shoulder seams. Press seams open. Trim seam allowance of facing to ¼" (6 mm) to eliminate bulk. Do not finish seams. Finish outer edge of facing.

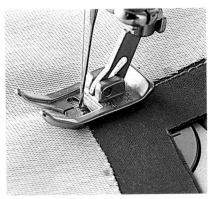

3) Stitch right side of facing to right side of garment, matching markings and shoulder seams. Shorten stitch length 1" (2.5 cm) from each corner and stitch to corner. Stop with needle in fabric.

4) Pivot at corner by raising presser foot and turning fabric around needle. Lower presser foot and stitch with short stitches for 1" (2.5 cm). Reset to regular stitch length and continue.

5) Clip into corners all the way to the reinforcement stitching. Grade seam allowances, turn, understitch and tack as shown in steps 7, 10, 11 and 12 on pages 96 and 97.

How to Sew a Curved Neckline (using nonfusible interfacing)

1) Join interfacing sections with lapped seams. Stitch and finish garment shoulder seams. Machine-baste interfacing to wrong side of garment, ½" (1.3 cm) from edge. Trim interfacing close to stitching. Trim outer edge ½" (1.3 cm).

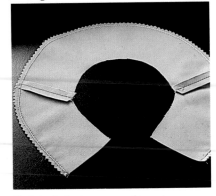

2) Stitch facings together at shoulder seams, trimming seam allowances to ¼" (6 mm). Press seams open, but do not finish. Finish outer edge of facing.

3) Stitch right side of facing to right side of garment. Grade and clip seam allowances of curves as shown in steps 7 and 8 on page 96. Press, understitch and tack facing as shown in steps 10 to 12 on page 97.

How to Sew a Pointed Collar (nonfusible interfacing)

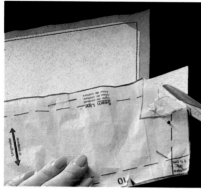

1) Trim corners of interfacing diagonally just inside seamline. Machine-baste interfacing to wrong side of upper collar, ½" (1.3 cm) from edge. Trim interfacing close to stitching.

2) Trim a scant ⅛" (3 mm) from outer edges of undercollar. This keeps undercollar from rolling to right side after collar is stitched to the neckline. Pin right sides of collar and undercollar together with outer edges even.

3) Stitch on seamline, taking one or two short stitches diagonally across each corner instead of making a sharp pivot. This makes a neater point when the collar is turned.

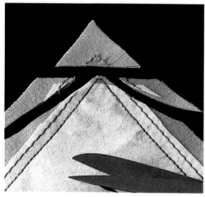

4) Trim corners, first across the point, close to stitching, then at an angle to the seam on each side of the point.

5) Grade seam allowances by trimming undercollar seam allowance to ⅛" (3 mm) and collar to ¼" (6 mm).

6) Press seam open on a point presser. Turn collar right side out.

7) Push points out gently with a point turner.

8) Press collar flat, rolling seam slightly to the underside so it will not show on finished collar.

How to Sew a Round Collar (using fusible interfacing)

1) Trim seam allowances from fusible interfacing and fuse to wrong side of upper collar, following manufacturer's instructions on package.

2) Trim scant ⅛" (3 mm) from outside edge of undercollar, as for pointed collar (page 99). Stitch right sides of collar and facing together, using shorter stitches on curves.

3) Trim seam allowances close to stitching line, using pinking shears (**1**). Or, grade and clip seam allowances (**2**). Press seam open, even though seam is enclosed. This flattens stitching line and makes collar easier to turn.

How to Sew and Attach a Collar (without a facing)

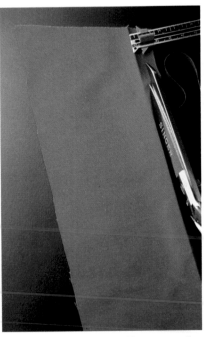

1) Staystitch neck edge of garment. Clip seam allowance up to stitching line so that curve will straighten to meet edge of collar.

2) Hold seam at each end and stretch into a straight line. The seam should not curl or pucker if there are enough clips and they are deep enough.

3) Press under seam allowance of upper collar along neck edge. Trim pressed seam allowance to ¼" (6 mm).

How to Sew and Attach a Collar (without a facing) Continued

4) Stitch right sides of collar and facing together as directed in step 3, page 99.

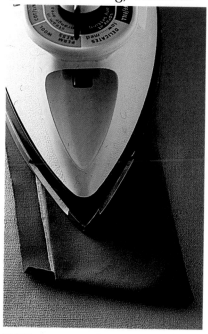

5) Trim, turn and press collar as directed for round or pointed collar (page 99 or 100).

6) Pin and stitch *undercollar only* to neckline edge, securing stitching at both ends. Trim seam allowances to ⅜" (1 cm).

7) Clip undercollar curves to stitching line. Press the seam toward the collar.

8) Pin the folded and trimmed edge of upper collar over seam allowances so the fold meets the stitching line.

9) Slipstitch (page 57) folded edge to seamline.

Waistbands

Because a waistband supports the entire garment, it must be a strong and sturdy outer edge finish. A basic waistband for skirts and pants is cut on the lengthwise grain of the fabric where there is the least amount of stretch. The waistband is stabilized with interfacing, doubled and sewn to the waistline edge, enclosing the seam allowance.

Most waistbands call for a turned-under edge as a finish on the inside. A faster, less bulky method requires changing the pattern layout so the waistband pattern is cut with one long edge on the selvage. Because the selvage does not ravel, a turned-under edge is not necessary. This method can be stitched entirely by machine. To further eliminate bulk, face waistbands of heavy fabrics with a lightweight fabric or grosgrain ribbon.

Cut a waistband long enough for adequate ease and overlap allowance. The length should equal your waist measurement plus 2¾" (7 cm). The extra amount includes ½" (1.3 cm) for ease, 1¼" (3.2 cm) for seam allowances, and 1" (2.5 cm) for overlap. The width should be twice the desired finished width plus 1¼" (3.2 cm) for seam allowances.

How to Sew a Waistband (selvage method)

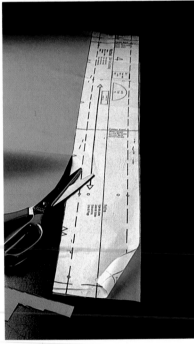

1) Cut waistband on the lengthwise grain, placing the cutting line of one long edge on the selvage.

2) Cut length of purchased fusible waistband interfacing according to pattern, cutting off ends at stitching line so interfacing does not extend into seam allowances.

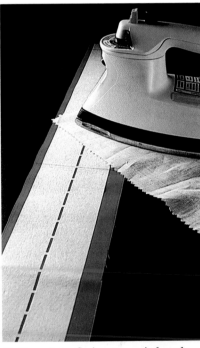

3) Fuse interfacing to waistband, with wider side of interfacing toward selvage edge. Interfacing should be placed so there is a ⅝" (1.5 cm) seam allowance on the notched edge (seam allowance on selvage edge will be narrower).

4) Pin right side of notched edge of waistband to right side of garment, matching notches. Stitch a ⅝" (1.5 cm) seam.

5) Turn waistband up. Press seam allowance toward waistband.

6) Grade the seam allowances to ¼" (6 mm) on the waistband and ⅛" (3 mm) on the garment to eliminate bulk.

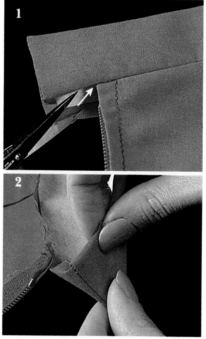

7) Fold waistband on interfacing center foldline so waistband is *wrong* side out. Stitch ⅝" (1.5 cm) seam on each end. Trim seam allowances to ¼" (6 mm). Diagonally trim corners.

8) Turn waistband right side out. **(1)** On underlap side, diagonally clip from selvage edge to corner (arrow). **(2)** Tuck seam allowance, from edge of underlap to end of clip, up into waistband. Fold clipped corner under at an angle.

9) Pin selvage edge of waistband in place. From right side of garment, stitch in the ditch of waistline seam or topstitch ¼" (6 mm) above the seam, catching selvage edge in stitching. Edgestitch lower edge of underlap (arrow) when using stitch-in-ditch method.

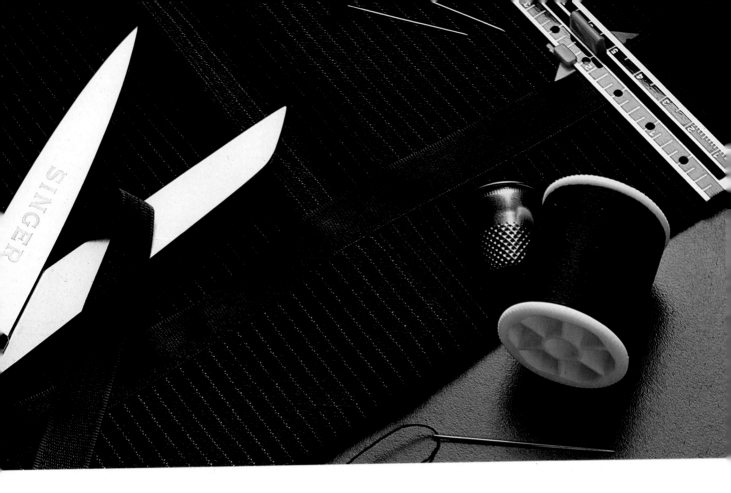

Hems

Unless a hem is decorative, it should be virtually invisible from the right side. Use thread the same shade as, or slightly darker than, your fabric.

When hemming by hand, pick up only one or two threads from the outer fabric in each stitch. Do not pull the thread too tight during stitching. This causes the hem to look puckered or lumpy. Press carefully; overpressing creates a ridge along the edge of the hem.

The width of the hem is determined by the fabric and garment style. A hem allowance of up to 3" (7.5 cm) may be given for a straight garment; 1½" to 2" (3.8 to 5 cm) for a flared one. Sheer fabrics, no matter what the style, are usually finished with a narrow, rolled hem. A narrow hem on soft knits helps keep them from sagging. Machine-stitched and topstitched hems are fast and permanent.

Before hemming, let the garment hang for 24 hours, especially if it has a bias or circular hem. Try the garment on over the undergarments you will wear with it. Check to be sure it fits and hangs correctly. Wear shoes, and a belt if the garment is to be belted.

Hemlines are usually marked with the help of a second person using a pin marker or yardstick. Mark the hemline with pins or chalk all around the garment, making sure the distance from the floor to the hemline remains equal. Stand in a normal position and have the helper move around the hem. Pin hem up, and try on the garment in front of a full-length mirror to double check that it is parallel to the floor.

Pants hems cannot be marked from the floor up, as skirts and dresses are. For standard-length pants, the bottom of the pants leg should rest on the shoe in front and slope down slightly toward the back. Pin up the hem on both legs, and try on in front of a mirror to check the length.

Before stitching, finish the raw edges of the hem to keep the fabric from raveling and to provide an anchor for the hemming stitch. Select the hem finish (opposite) and stitch that is appropriate to the fabric and the garment. (See hand stitches, page 57.)

Blindstitching by machine makes a fast, sturdy hem on woven and knit fabrics. Many sewing machines have this built-in stitch. A special foot or stitching guide makes blindstitching easy.

Seam binding or lace (above) provides a finish suitable for fabrics which ravel, such as wool, tweed or linen. Lap seam binding ¼" (6 mm) over the hem edge on the right side of the fabric. Edgestitch the binding in place, overlapping ends at a seamline. Use woven seam binding for straight hems, stretch lace for curved hems and knits. Hem light to mediumweight fabrics with the catchstitch, bulky fabrics with the blindstitch.

Hem Finishes & Stitches

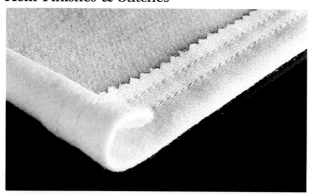

Topstitched hem finishes the raw edge and hems the garment all in one step. Turn up hem 1½" (3.8 cm) and pin in place. For ravelly fabrics, pink or turn under raw edge. On right side, topstitch 1" (2.5 cm) from folded edge. Above, a second row of topstitching is applied as a design detail.

Twin-needle stitched hem is suitable for knits and casual styles. The twin needle produces two closely-spaced parallel lines of stitching on the right side and a zigzag-type stitch on the wrong side. Turn hem up desired amount and stitch through both layers from right side, using seam guide. Trim excess hem allowance after stitching.

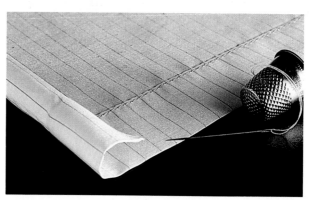

Zigzag finish is appropriate for knits and fabrics that ravel, because the stitch gives with the fabric. Stitch close to raw edge with zigzag stitch of medium width and length. Trim close to stitching. Hem with a blindstitch, blind catchstitch or machine blindstitch.

Turned and stitched finish is appropriate for woven lightweight fabrics. Turn raw edge under ¼" (6 mm). Stitch near the edge of the fold. Hem using slipstitch or blindstitch.

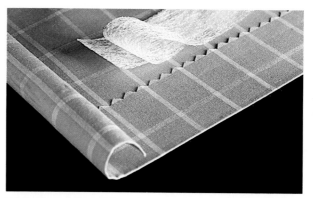

Bound hem finish is appropriate for heavy woolens and fabrics that ravel easily. Finish raw edge of hem in double-fold bias tape or Hong Kong finish (page 67). Hem with blindstitch or blind catchstitch. Be careful not to pull hemming thread too tight or fabric will pucker.

Pinked and fused hem is a fast and easy finish for lightweight woven fabrics. Apply a fusible web strip between the hem and the garment. Steam press, following manufacturer's instructions. Most fusible webs require 15 seconds of heat and steam applied in each section of the hem for permanent bonding.

How to Turn Up a Hem

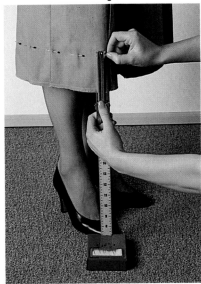

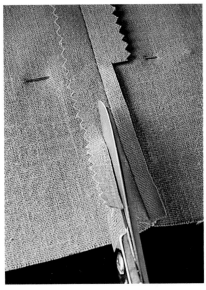

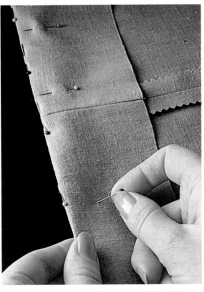

1) Mark garment an even distance from the floor using pins or chalk, and a yardstick or skirt marker. Have your helper move around you so you do not need to shift position or posture. Place marks every 2" (5 cm).

2) Trim seam allowances in hem by half to reduce bulk. Trim seams from bottom of garment to hem stitching line only.

3) Fold hem up along marked line, inserting pins at right angles to the fold at regular intervals. Try on garment to check length.

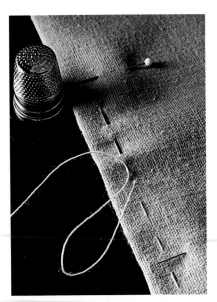

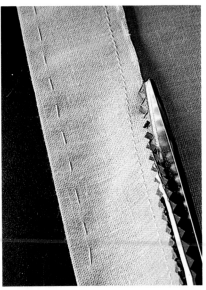

4) Hand-baste ¼" (6 mm) from folded edge. Press edge lightly, easing hem to fit garment.

5) Measure and mark the desired hem depth, adding ¼" (6 mm) for edge finish. Work on ironing board or table, using a seam gauge to ensure even marking.

6) Trim excess hem allowance along markings. Finish raw edge according to fabric type (page 105). Pin finished edge to garment, matching seams and center lines.

How to Sew a Curved Hem

1) Prepare hem as shown opposite, but do not finish raw edge. Curved hems have extra fullness which must be eased to fit garment. Loosen machine tension and easestitch ¼" (6 mm) from edge, stopping and starting at a seamline.

2) Draw up bobbin thread by pulling up a loop with a pin at intervals, easing fullness to smoothly fit garment shape. Do not draw hem in too much, or it will pull against garment when finished. Press hem over a press mitt to smooth out some fullness.

3) Finish raw edge using zigzag stitching, bias tape, seam binding or pinking. Pin hem edge to garment, matching seams and center lines. Hem using machine blindstitch or appropriate hand hemming stitch.

How to Machine Blindstitch

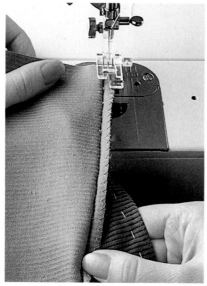

1) Prepare hemline as shown, opposite. Hand-baste hem to garment, ¼" (6 mm) from raw edge. Adjust machine to blindstitch setting and attach blindstitch foot. Select zigzag width and stitch length according to weight and texture of fabric. The stitch taken into the garment is adjustable from ¹⁄₁₆" to ⅛" (1.5 to 3 mm).

2) Place hem allowance face down over feed of machine. Fold bulk of garment back to basting line. The soft fold should rest against the right part of the foot (arrow). Some machines use a regular zigzag foot with a blindstitch hemming guide attached.

3) Stitch along hem close to the fold, catching garment only in zigzag stitch. While stitching, guide hem edge in a straight line and feed soft fold against the right part of the hemming foot or the edge of the guide. Open out hem and press flat.

Closures

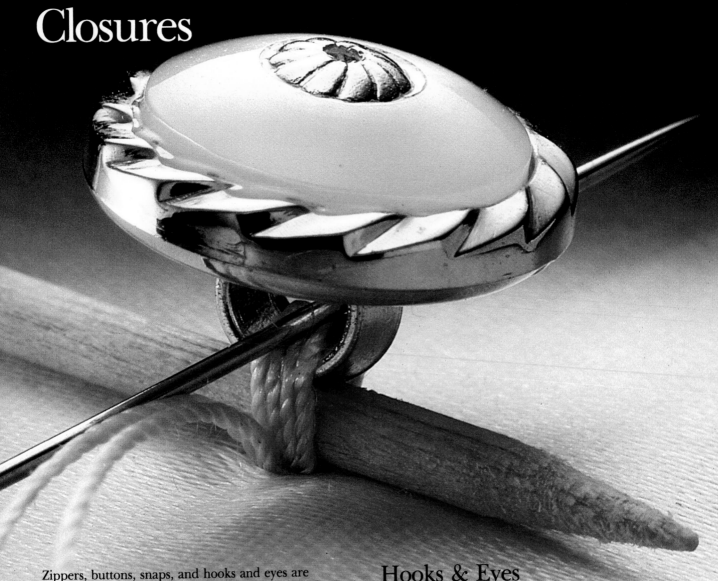

Zippers, buttons, snaps, and hooks and eyes are usually meant to be as inconspicuous as possible, but are sometimes used as decorative details. A stylish button, colorful separating zipper or pearlized gripper snap can make a definite fashion statement.

Select the closure according to the style of garment and amount of strain that will be put on the opening. For example, a heavy-duty hook and eye closure (opposite) can better withstand the strain on a pants waistband than ordinary hooks and eyes. The back of the pattern envelope specifies the type and size of closures to purchase.

Because closures are under strain, it is important to reinforce the garment area where they are placed. Seam allowances or facings provide light reinforcement. Other closure areas should be reinforced with interfacing.

For sewing on buttons, snaps, and hooks and eyes, use an all-purpose thread, and sharps or crewel needles. For heavyweight fabrics or for closures that are under considerable strain, use heavy-duty, or topstitching and buttonhole twist thread.

Hooks & Eyes

Hooks and eyes are strong closures and come in several types. Regular, general-purpose hooks and eyes are available in sizes 0 (fine) to 3 (heavy), in black or nickel finishes. They have either straight or round eyes. Straight eyes are used where garment edges overlap, such as on a waistband. Round eyes are used where two edges meet, such as at the neckline above a centered zipper. Thread loops (opposite) can be used in place of round metal eyes on delicate fabrics or in locations where metal eyes would be too conspicuous. Button loops and belt carriers are made using the same technique, starting with longer foundation stitches.

Heavy-duty hooks and eyes are stronger than regular hooks and eyes, to withstand greater strain. Available in black or nickel finishes, they are used only for lapped areas. Large, plain or covered hooks and eyes are available for coats and jackets. These are attractive enough to be visible and strong enough to hold heavy fabric.

How to Attach Waistband Hooks & Eyes

1) Position heavy-duty hook on underside of waistband overlap, about ⅛" (3 mm) from inside edge. Tack hook in place with three or four stitches through each hole. Do not stitch through to right side of garment.

2) Lap hook side over underlap to mark position of eye. Insert straight pins through holes to mark position. Tack in place with three or four stitches in each hole.

Round hook and eye is used for waistbands which do not overlap. Position hook as for heavy-duty hook. Tack through both holes and at end of hook. Position eye so it extends slightly over inside edge of fabric (garments edges should butt together). Tack in place.

How to Make Thread Eyes

 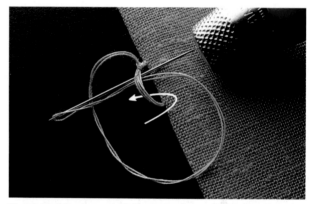

1) Insert needle with double strand of thread at edge of fabric. Take two foundation stitches the desired length of the eye. These are the anchor on which blanket stitch is worked.

2) Work blanket stitch by bringing eye of needle under foundation stitches and through the loop.

3) Bring needle through loop, pulling loop tight against foundation stitches. Work blanket stitch along entire length of foundation stitches.

4) Secure stitching by taking two small backstitches. Trim threads.

Buttonholes

The standards of a well-made buttonhole are:
1) Width is appropriate to the weight of the fabric and size of the buttonhole.
2) Ends are bar-tacked to prevent buttonhole from tearing under stress.
3) Stitches are evenly spaced on each side of the buttonhole.
4) Buttonhole is ⅛" (3 mm) longer than the button.
5) Stitches on each side are far enough apart so that the buttonhole can be cut open without cutting the stitches.
6) Ends have not been cut open accidentally.
7) Interfacing supporting the buttonhole matches the fashion fabric and is not obvious on the cut edges.
8) Buttonhole is on-grain; vertical buttonholes are perfectly parallel to the garment edge, horizontal buttonholes are at perfect right angles to the edge.

Horizontal buttonholes are the most secure, because they are not as apt to let buttons slip out. These buttonholes also absorb any pull against the closure with little, if any, distortion. Horizontal buttonholes should extend ⅛" (3 mm) beyond the button placement line, toward the edge of the garment. Be sure that the space from the center line to the finished edge of the garment is at least three-fourths the diameter of the button. With this spacing, the button will not extend beyond the edge when the garment is buttoned.

Vertical buttonholes are used on plackets and shirt bands. These are usually used with more and smaller buttons to help keep the closure secure. Vertical buttonholes are placed directly on the center front or center back line.

When a garment is buttoned, the button placement lines and center lines of both sides must match perfectly. If the overlap is more or less than the pattern indicates, the garment may not fit properly.

Spaces between buttonholes are generally equal. You may have to change the pattern buttonhole spacing if you have made pattern alterations that change the length or alter the bustline. Respacing may also be necessary if you have chosen buttons that are larger or smaller than the pattern indicates. Buttonholes should be spaced so they occur in the areas of greatest stress. When they are incorrectly spaced, the closing gaps and spoils the garment's appearance.

For front openings, place buttonholes at the neck and the fullest part of the bust. Place a buttonhole at the waist for coats, overblouses and princess-seamed dresses or jackets. To reduce bulk, do not place a buttonhole at the waistline of a tucked-in blouse or belted dress. Buttons and buttonholes should end about 5" to 6" (12.5 to 15 cm) above the hemline of a dress, skirt or coatdress.

To evenly respace buttonholes, mark the locations of the top and bottom buttons. Measure the distance between them. Divide that measurement by one less than the number of buttons to be used. The result is the distance between buttonholes. After marking, try on the garment, making sure the buttonholes are placed correctly for your figure. Adjust as necessary.

How to Determine Buttonhole Length

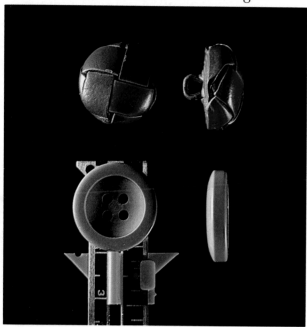

Measure width and height of button to be used. The sum of these measurements plus ⅛" (3 mm) for finishing the ends of the buttonhole is the correct length for a machine-worked buttonhole. The buttonhole must be large enough to button easily, yet snug enough so the garment stays closed.

Test proposed buttonhole. First, make a slash in a scrap of fabric the length of the buttonhole minus the extra ⅛" (3 mm). If button passes through easily, length is correct. Next, make a practice buttonhole with garment, facing and interfacing. Check length, stitch width, density of stitching and buttonhole cutting space.

How to Mark Buttonholes

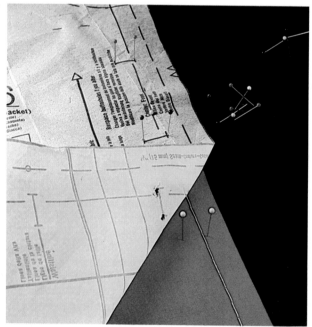

Place pattern tissue on top of garment, aligning pattern seamline with garment opening edge. Insert pins straight down through tissue and fabric at both ends of each buttonhole marking. Remove pattern carefully, pulling tissue over heads of pins.

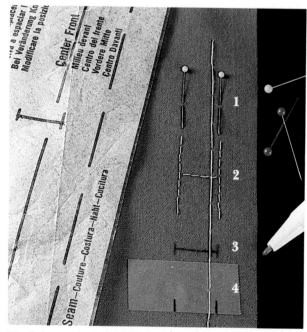

Mark buttonholes using one of the following methods: **(1)** Secure pins. **(2)** Machine or hand-baste between pins and along ends. **(3)** Use a water-soluble marking pen. **(4)** Place a piece of tape above the pins and mark buttonhole length with a pencil; test fabric first to be sure tape does not mar it.

Machine-made Buttonholes

Machine-made buttonholes are appropriate for most garments, especially those which are casual or tailored. There are four types: *built-in* (usually two or four-step), *overedge, one-step* and *universal attachment*. Always make a test buttonhole with appropriate interfacing before making the buttonholes on your garment. The test buttonhole also reminds you at which point your machine begins the buttonhole stitching, so you can position fabric correctly.

1) **Built-in buttonholes** are made with a combination of zigzag stitching and bar tacks. Most zigzag machines have a built-in mechanism that stitches this type of buttonhole in two or four steps. The four steps are: zigzag forward, bar tack, zigzag in reverse, bar tack. A two-step buttonhole combines a forward or backward motion with a bar tack. Consult your machine manual for specific directions, because each machine varies. The advantage of this buttonhole is that it allows you to adjust the density of the zigzag to suit the fabric and size of the buttonhole. Use spaced zigzag stitches on bulky or loosely woven fabrics, closer stitches on sheer or delicate fabrics.

2) **Overedge buttonholes** are an adaptation of the built-in or one-step buttonhole. This buttonhole is stitched with a narrow zigzag, cut open and then stitched a second time, so the cut edge is overedged with zigzag stitches. The overedge buttonhole looks like a hand-worked buttonhole. It is a good choice when the interfacing is not a close color match to the fashion fabric.

3) **One-step buttonholes** are stitched all in one step, using a special foot and a built-in stitch available on some machines. They can be stitched with a standard-width zigzag, or a narrow zigzag for lightweight fabrics. The button is placed in a carrier in back of the attachment and guides the stitching, so the buttonhole fits the button perfectly. A lever near the needle is pulled down and stops the foward motion of the machine when the buttonhole reaches the correct length. All buttonholes are of uniform length, so placement is the only marking necessary.

4) **Universal attachment buttonholes** are made with an attachment which will fit any machine, including a straight-stitch machine. The attachment has a *template* which determines the size of the buttonhole. This method also offers the advantage of uniform buttonhole length and adjustable zigzag width. The *keyhole* buttonhole, used on tailored garments or heavy fabrics, can be made using this attachment. The keyhole at one end of the buttonhole provides space for the shank.

If buttonholes do not have to be respaced because of pattern alterations, make the buttonholes after attaching and finishing the facings but before joining to another garment section. This way there is less bulk and weight to handle at the machine.

How to Make Buttonholes

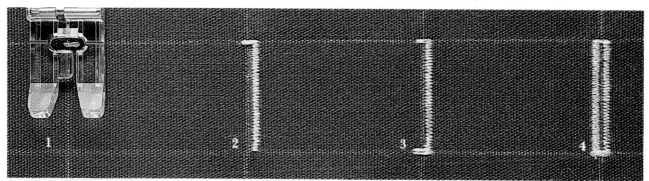

Built-in buttonholes (four-step). Place fabric under buttonhole foot, aligning starting point with needle and centering foot over center marking. (Steps are pictured separately above, but buttonhole is stitched continuously, moving machine to new setting at each step.) **1)** Set dial or lever selector at first step. Slowly stitch 3 or 4 stitches across end to form bar tack. **2)**

Stitch one side. Some machines stitch left side first, others stitch right side. Stitch only as far as marked end. **3)** Stitch 3 or 4 stitches across end to form second bar tack. **4)** Stitch other side to complete buttonhole. Stop sewing when stitching reaches the first bar tack. Return to starting position and make one or two fastening stitches.

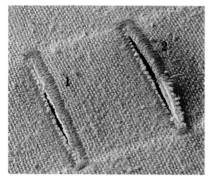

Overedge buttonhole. 1) Stitch buttonhole with narrow zigzag. Cut buttonhole open and trim loose threads. **2)** Reposition buttonhole in exact position as first stitching. Adjust zigzag width to wider stitch. Stitch second time with zigzag going over cut edge of buttonhole.

One-step buttonhole. Place button in attachment carrier. Check machine manual for proper stitch setting. Buttonhole is made the correct length and stitching will stop automatically. Cut open and stitch buttonhole a second time to add an overedge finish.

Universal attachment buttonhole. Attach buttonhole attachment as instructed in manual. Select template of proper size to fit button. For sturdier reinforced buttonhole, stitch around the buttonhole a second time.

How to Open a Buttonhole

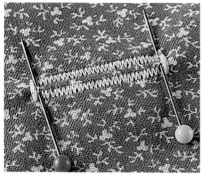

1) Insert straight pins at each end of buttonhole in front of bar tacks to prevent cutting through ends.

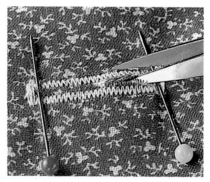

2) Insert point of a small, sharp scissors or seam ripper into center of buttonhole and carefully cut toward one end, then the other.

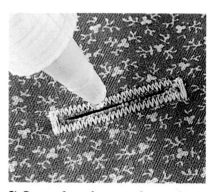

3) Strengthen the cut edge and prevent raveling by applying liquid fray preventer to the edge. Test on a sample first.

Buttons

More than any other closure, buttons allow you to individualize your garment. Buttons can be decorative as well as functional. There are two basic kinds of buttons, *sew-through* and *shank* buttons, but the variations on these two types are endless.

Sew-through buttons are usually flat, with two or four holes. When they are merely decorative, they can be sewn so they lie directly against the garment. On all other applications, sew-through buttons need a thread shank. A *shank* raises the button from the garment surface, allowing space for the layers of fabric to fit smoothly when it is buttoned.

Shank buttons have their own shanks on the underside. Choose shank buttons for heavier fabrics, as well as when using button loops or thread loops.

When selecting buttons, consider color, style, weight and care.

Color. The color of buttons is usually matched to the fabric, but interesting fashion looks can be achieved with coordinating or contrasting colors. If you are unable to find an appropriate color match, make your own fabric-covered buttons with a kit.

Style. Select small, delicate buttons for feminine garments; clean, classic styles for tailored clothes; novelty buttons for children's clothes. Rhinestone buttons add sparkle to a velvet garment. Try leather or metal buttons with corduroy and wool tweeds.

Weight. Match lightweight buttons to lightweight fabrics. Heavy buttons will pull and distort lightweight fabrics. Heavyweight fabrics need buttons that are bigger or look weightier.

Care. Choose buttons that can be cared for in the same manner as the garment, either washable or dry-cleanable.

The back of the pattern envelope tells you how many and what size buttons to purchase. Try not to go more than 1/8" (3 mm) smaller or larger than the pattern specifies. Buttons that are too small or too large may not be in proper proportion to the edge of the garment. Button sizes are listed in inches, millimeters and *lines*. For example, a 1/2" button is also listed as 13 mm and line 20; a 3/4" button, as 19 mm and line 30.

When shopping for buttons, bring a swatch of fabric with you to assure a good match. Cut a small slit in the fabric so a button on the card can be slipped through, giving you a better idea of how it will look when finished.

Sew on buttons with doubled all-purpose thread for lightweight fabrics, and heavy-duty or buttonhole twist for heavier fabrics. When attaching several buttons, double the sewing thread so you are sewing with four strands at once. This way, two stitches will secure the button.

How to Mark Button Location

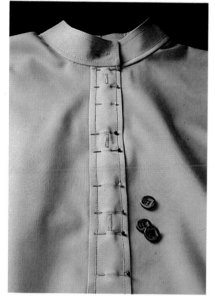

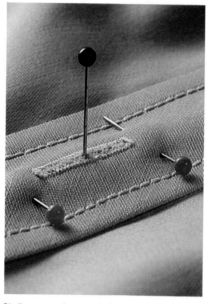

1) Mark button placement by lapping the buttonhole side of garment over the button side, matching center lines. Pin garment closed between buttonholes.

2) Insert pin straight through buttonhole and into bottom layer of fabric. For vertical buttonholes, insert pin in center of buttonhole. For horizontal buttonholes, insert pin at edge closest to outer edge of garment.

3) Carefully lift buttonhole over pin. Insert threaded needle at point of pin to sew on button. Mark and sew buttons one at a time, buttoning previous buttons for accurate marking.

How to Sew on a Shank Button

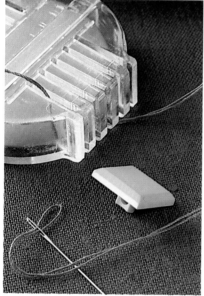

1) Cut a length of thread 30" (76 cm) long and run it through beeswax to strengthen it. Fold thread in half. Thread folded end through a crewel needle. Knot cut ends of thread. Position button at pin mark on the garment center line, placing shank hole parallel to the buttonhole.

2) Secure thread on right side with small stitch under button. Bring needle through shank hole. Insert needle down into fabric and pull through. Repeat, taking four to six stitches through the shank.

3) Secure thread in fabric under button by making a knot or taking several small stitches. Clip thread ends. If a shank button is used on a heavy fabric, it may also need a thread shank. Follow instructions for making a thread shank on a sew-through button, page 116.

How to Hand Sew a Sew-through Button

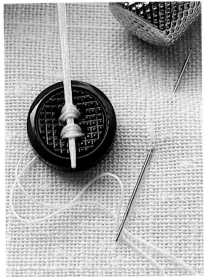

1) Thread needle as for shank button (page 115) and position button at pin mark. Place holes in button so they line up parallel to buttonhole. Bring needle through fabric from underside and up through one hole in button. Insert needle into another hole and through the fabric layers.

2) Slip a toothpick, match or sewing machine needle between thread and button to form shank. Take three or four stitches through each pair of holes. Bring needle and thread to right side under button. Remove toothpick.

3) Wind thread two or three times around button stitches to form shank. Secure thread on right side under button by making a knot or taking several small stitches. Clip threads close to knot.

How to Machine Sew a Sew-through Button

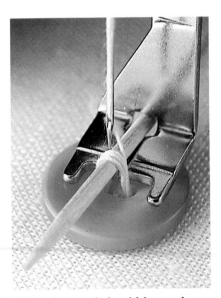

1) Attach button foot and special plate to cover feed, or drop feed. Button will be stitched with close zigzag stitching. Regulate stitch width and tension as directed in machine manual.

2) Position button under foot. Lower needle into center of one button hole by turning handwheel towards you. Lower presser foot. Turn handwheel until needle rises out of button and is just above foot. Insert match or toothpick to form shank.

3) Set zigzag stitch width regulator so that stitch width equals the space between holes in button. Proceed slowly until you are sure you have the correct width. Take six or more zigzag stitches. Secure the stitching as directed in your machine manual.

Snaps

Snaps are available as regular sew-on snaps, gripper-type snaps or snap tape.

Sew-on snaps are suitable for areas where there is little strain, such as at the neckline or waistline to hold the facing edge flat when buttons are used, at the waistline of blouses, or at the pointed end of a waistband fastened with hooks and eyes. Sew-on snaps consist of two parts: a ball and a socket. Select a size that is strong enough to be secure, but not too heavy for the fabric.

Gripper-type snaps are attached with a special plier tool or a hammer. They have more holding power than a sew-in snap and will show on the right side of the garment. Gripper snaps can replace button and buttonhole closures in sportswear.

Snap tape consists of snaps attached to pieces of tape. The tape is stitched to the garment with a zipper foot. Snap tape is used in sportswear, home decorating, and for the inside seam of infant's and toddler's pants.

How to Attach Sew-on Snaps

1) Position ball half of snap on wrong side of overlap section, ⅛" to ¼" (3 to 6 mm) from the edge so it will not show on the right side. Stitch in place through each hole, using single strand of thread. Stitch through facing and interfacing only, not through to right side of garment. Secure thread with two tiny stitches.

2) Mark position of socket half of snap on right side of underlap section. Use one of the following methods: If there is a hole in center of ball half, insert pin from right side through hole and into underlap section. If there is no hole in ball, rub tailor's chalk on ball and press firmly against underlap.

3) Position center of socket half over marking. Stitch in place in same manner as ball half, except stitch through all layers of fabric.

117

Zippers

Down the back, up the front, on sleeves, pockets or pants legs — zippers provide closings on a variety of fashion features. *Conventional* zippers are most often used. They are closed at one end and sewn into a seam. *Invisible, separating,* and *heavy-duty* zippers are available for special uses.

The pattern specifies the type and length zipper to buy. When selecting a zipper, choose a color that closely matches your fabric. Also consider the weight of the zipper in relation to the weight of the fabric. Choose synthetic coil zippers for lightweight fabrics, because these zippers are lighter and more flexible than metal zippers. If you cannot find a zipper of the correct length, buy one that is slightly longer than you need and shorten it using the directions on the opposite page.

There are several ways to insert a zipper. The one you choose depends on the type of garment and the location of the zipper in the garment. The following pages contain instructions for the *lapped, centered* and *fly-front* applications for conventional zippers, and two methods for inserting separating zippers. There are variations of each of these applications. Methods shown here are quick and easy, featuring timesaving tools such as fabric glue stick and transparent tape.

Close the zipper and press out the creases before inserting it in the garment. If the zipper has a cotton tape and will be applied in a washable garment, preshrink it in hot water before application. This will prevent the zipper from puckering when the garment is laundered. For best appearance, the final stitching on the outside of the garment should be straight and an even distance from the seamline. Stitch both sides of the zipper from bottom to top, and turn the pull tab up to make it easier to stitch past the slider.

Parts of the Zipper

Top stop is the small metal bracket at the top that prevents the slider from running off the tape.

Slider and pull tab is the mechanism that operates the zipper. It locks the teeth together to close the zipper and unlocks the teeth to open the zipper.

Tape is the fabric strip on which the teeth or coil are fastened. The tape is sewn to the garment.

Teeth or coil is the part of the zipper that locks together when the slider runs along it. It may be made of nylon, polyester or metal.

Bottom stop is the bracket at the bottom of the zipper where the slider rests when the zipper is open. Separating zippers have a bottom stop which splits into two parts to allow the zipper to be completely opened.

Separating zippers in jackets and vests can be inserted with zipper teeth covered or exposed. A decorative sport zipper with plastic teeth is lightweight yet sturdy, for active sportswear.

Applications for Conventional Zippers

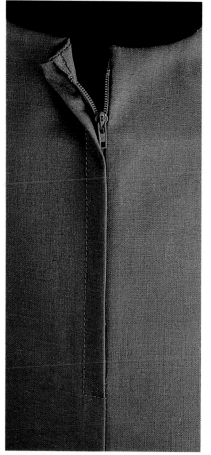

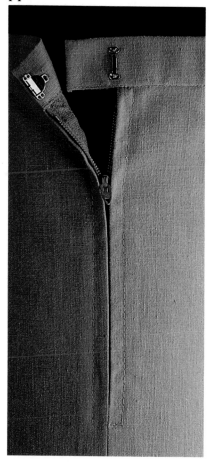

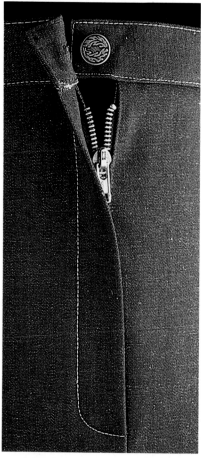

Lapped application totally conceals the zipper, making it a good choice for zippers which do not perfectly match the fabric color. It is most often used in side seam closings of dresses, skirts and pants.

Centered application is most frequently used for center front and center back closings. Attach facings *before* inserting the zipper. Waistbands should be applied *after* the zipper is inserted.

Fly-front zipper is often found on pants and skirts, and occasionally on coats and jackets. Use the fly-front application only when the pattern calls for it, because it requires the wider underlap and facing included in the pattern.

How to Shorten a Zipper

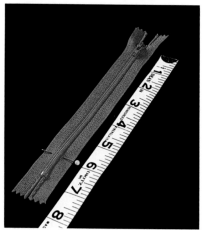

1) Measure desired length along the coil, beginning at top stop. Mark with pin.

2) Machine zigzag across the coil at pin to form new bottom stop.

3) Cut off excess zipper and tape. Insert zipper as usual, stitching slowly across coil at bottom.

How to Insert a Lapped Zipper

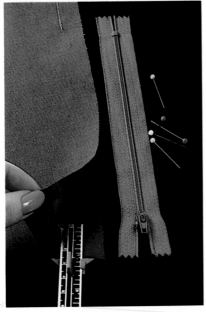

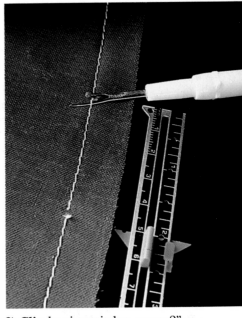

1) Turn the garment to the wrong side. Check seam opening to make sure top edges are even. Length of opening should be equal to length of zipper *coil* plus 1" (2.5 cm). Pin seam from bottom of opening to top of garment.

2) Machine-baste on seamline from bottom of the opening to top of the garment, removing pins as you stitch.

3) Clip basting stitches every 2" (5 cm) to make basting easier to remove after zipper is inserted.

7) Close zipper and turn face up. Smooth fabric away from zipper, forming narrow fold between zipper coil and basted seam.

8) Adjust zipper foot to left side of needle. Starting at bottom of zipper tape, stitch near edge of fold, through folded seam allowance and zipper tape.

9) Turn zipper over so face side is flat against seam. Make sure pull tab is turned up to lessen bulk while stitching. Pin in place.

4) Press seam open. If zipper is in side seam of skirt or pants, press seam over a press mitt or tailor's ham to retain shape of hipline.

5) Open zipper. Place face down on right-hand side of seam allowance (top of garment facing you). Position zipper coil directly on seamline with top stop 1" (2.5 cm) below cut edge. Turn pull tab up. Pin, glue or tape right-hand side of zipper tape in place.

6) Replace presser foot with zipper foot and adjust it to right side of needle. Machine-baste close to edge of coil, stitching from bottom to top of zipper with edge of zipper foot against coil. Remove pins as you stitch.

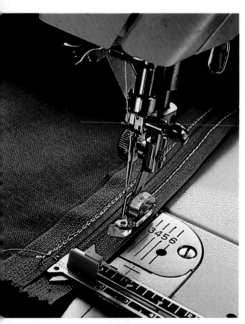

10) Adjust zipper foot to right side of needle. Starting at top of zipper, machine-baste through tape and seam allowance only. This holds seam allowance in place for the final stitching.

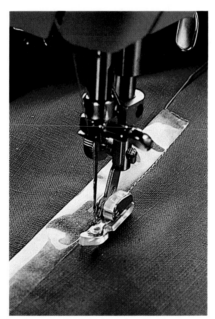

11) Topstitch ½" (1.3 cm) from seam on outside of garment. To aid straight stitching, use ½" (1.3 cm) transparent tape and stitch along edge. Starting at seamline, stitch across bottom of zipper, pivot at edge of tape and continue to top cut edge.

12) Remove tape. Pull thread at bottom of zipper to wrong side and knot. Remove machine basting in seam. Press, using a press cloth to protect fabric from shine. Trim zipper tape even with top edge of garment.

How to Insert a Centered Zipper (using glue stick)

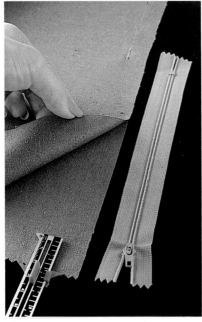

1) Turn garment to the wrong side. Check seam opening to make sure top edges are even. Length of opening should be equal to length of zipper *coil* plus 1" (2.5 cm).

2) Pin seam from bottom of opening to top of garment.

3) Machine-baste on seamline from bottom of opening to top of garment. Clip basting stitches every 2" (5 cm) to make basting easier to remove.

7) Spread garment flat, right side up. Mark bottom stop of zipper with pin. Use transparent or perforated marking tape, ½" (1.3 cm) wide and same length as zipper. Place down center of seamline. Do not use tape on napped or delicate fabrics.

8) Replace presser foot with zipper foot and adjust to left of needle. Topstitch zipper from right side, beginning at seam at bottom of tape. Stitch across bottom of zipper; pivot at edge of tape. Stitch up left side of zipper to top cut edge, using edge of tape as a guide.

9) Adjust the zipper foot to right side of needle. Begin at seam at bottom of tape and stitch across bottom. Pivot and stitch up right side of zipper, using edge of tape as a guide.

4) Press seam open. Finish raw edges if fabric ravels easily.

5) Apply glue stick (page 20) lightly on face side of zipper.

6) Place zipper face down on seam, with zipper coil directly on seamline and top stop 1" (2.5 cm) below cut edge (keep pull tab up). Press with fingers to secure zipper. Let glue dry for a few minutes.

10) Pull both threads at bottom to wrong side. Tie all four threads, using pin to pull knot close to zipper (page 59). Clip threads.

11) Turn garment to right side. Remove tape. Carefully remove machine basting in seamline.

12) Press, using a press cloth to protect fabric from shine. Trim zipper tape even with the top edge of the garment.

How to Insert a Fly-front Zipper

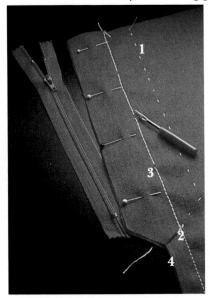  

1) Mark zipper topstitching line on right side with hand basting or non-permanent marking (**1**). Stitch front crotch seam, backstitching at marking for end of zipper placket (**2**). Machine-baste seam closed (**3**). Clip basting stitches every 2" (5 cm). Clip seam allowances below fly facings (**4**). Press facings open.

2) Fold right-hand fly facing (top edge facing you) under ¼" to ½" (6 mm to 1.3 cm) from center front. Place folded edge along coil with top stop 1" (2.5 cm) below top edge. Pin or baste in place.

3) Replace presser foot with zipper foot and adjust to left of needle. Stitch close to the fold, starting at bottom of zipper.

4) Turn zipper face down over *left* fly facing. Turn pull tab up and bulk of garment out of the way. Adjust zipper foot to right of needle. Starting at top of zipper, stitch through tape and fly facing, ¼" (6 mm) from zipper coil.

5) Spread garment flat, wrong side up. Pin left fly extension to garment front. Turn garment to right side and repin fly facing. Remove pins from inside.

6) Stitch on right side along marked topstitching line, with zipper foot to right of needle. Begin at seam at bottom of zipper and stitch to top of garment, removing pins as you come to them. Pull threads to inside and knot. Remove basting and marking. Press using a press cloth.

How to Insert a Covered Separating Zipper

1) Use basting tape, pins or glue to hold closed zipper, face up, under faced opening edges. Position pull tab ⅛" (3 mm) below neck seamline. Edges of the opening should meet at center of zipper, covering the teeth.

2) Open zipper. Turn ends of zipper tape under at top of garment. Pin in place.

3) Topstitch ⅜" (1 cm) from each opening edge, sewing through fabric and zipper tape. Stitch from bottom to top on each side, adjusting zipper foot to correct side.

How to Insert an Exposed Separating Zipper

 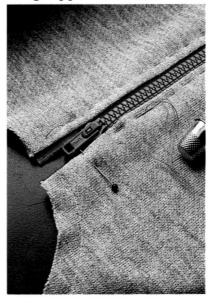 

1) Pin faced opening edges to closed zipper so that edges are close to but not covering zipper teeth, with pull tab ⅛" (3 mm) below neck seamline.

2) Baste zipper in place with tape ends extending above neck seamline. Turn ends of zipper tape under at top of garment if facing is already attached. Open zipper.

3) Topstitch close to opening edges on right side of garment, using zipper foot and stitching from bottom to top on each side. To hold zipper tape flat, add another line of stitching ¼" (6 mm) from first stitching line on each side.

Index